EARLY CHILDHOOD EDUCATION SERIES

Leslie Williams, Editor
Millie Almy, Senior Advisor

Advisory Board: Barbara T. Bowman, Harriet Cuffaro, Celia Genishi, Alice Sterling Honig, Elizabeth Jones, Gwen Morgan, David Weikart

Elinor Fitch Griffin, *Island of Childhood: Education in the Special World of Nursery School*

Sandra R. Curtis, *The Joy of Movement in Early Childhood*

Frances E. Kendall, *Diversity in the Classroom: A Multicultural Approach to the Evaluation of Young Children*

James T. Greenman and Robert W. Fuqua, editors, *Making Day Care Better: Training, Education, and the Process of Change*

Evelyn Weber, *Ideas Influencing Early Childhood Education: A Theoretical Analysis*

Constance Kazuko Kamii, *Young Children Reinvent Arithmetic: Implications of Piaget's Theory*

Nancy Balaban, *Starting School: From Separation to Independence (A Guide for Early Childhood Teachers)*

John Cleverley and D. C. Phillips, *Visions of Childhood: Influential Models from Locke to Spock*

Joseph J. Caruso and M. Temple Fawcett, *Supervision in Early Childhood Education: A Developmental Perspective*

Bernard Spodek, editor, *Today's Kindergarten: Exploring the Knowledge Base, Expanding the Curriculum*

To Allison, Anne, Dan,
Darryl, David, Helen, Hill,
Jane, Jon and Russ
—model children all.

Revised Edition

VISIONS OF CHILDHOOD
Influential Models from Locke to Spock

JOHN CLEVERLEY
University of Sydney

D. C. PHILLIPS
Stanford University

TEACHERS
COLLEGE
PRESS

Teachers College, Columbia University
New York and London

Published by Teachers College Press, 1234 Amsterdam Avenue
New York, N.Y.   10027

Library of Congress Cataloging in Publication Data

Cleverley, John F.
  Visions of childhood.

  Bibliography: p.
  Includes index.
    1. Education—Philosophy—History.   2. Children—
Social conditions.   3. Child rearing—History.   4. Child
rearing—Philosophy.   I. Phillips, D. C. (Denis Charles),
1938–   II. Title.
LA11.C545   1986   370′.1   85-30359
ISBN 0-8077-2801-2
ISBN 0-8077-2800-4 (pbk.)

Manufactured in the United States of America

91   90   89   3   4   5   6

CONTENTS

PREFACE   *vii*

1. ON SEEING CHILDREN THROUGHOUT HISTORY   *1*

2. THE CHILD AND THE ENVIRONMENT   *13*

3. THE FREE AND THE CONSTRAINED CHILD   *28*

4. THE CHILD AND THE SPECIES   *42*

5. THE LOSS OF INNOCENCE: THE FREUDIAN CHILD   *54*

6. THE AGES OF MAN: FROM GENESIS TO PIAGET   *80*

7. AN UPBRINGING FIT FOR SOCIETY: MARX AND DEWEY   *97*

8. THE CONDITIONED CHILD   *114*

9. THE THINKING MACHINE   *131*

10. POSTSCRIPT   *141*

NOTES   *147*

INDEX   *161*

ABOUT THE AUTHORS   *166*

PREFACE

THERE is a vast literature about children and their upbringing. The best-selling book in the Western world, after the Bible, is a handbook on child care. Each year, new books are produced by pediatricians, psychologists, historians, anthropologists. . . . Successful people from all walks of life write reminiscences of childhood, and growing up provides a favorite theme for novelists. Across the United States, tens of thousands of college students take courses on child development and are exposed to the classic works of the field. And, of course, hundreds of thousands of people become parents for the first time. Despite this interest in, and attention to, children, it is still not generally appreciated how a small number of theories—theories with sometimes controversial underpinnings—have decisively shaped the patterns of child rearing and the educational practices that have been adopted. Although dealing with children can initially provoke a great deal of anxiety, familiarity breeds confidence; the new parent or the young teacher quickly settles into a routine and may never realize that the practices that have been slipped into are based on assumptions that could be astounding if made explicit. (There is a parallel here to the American Constitution; when some of the underlying assumptions were taken out and expressed in modern language, most people asked to comment upon them not only failed to recognize the source, but strongly disagreed with them!)

Occasionally there are flashes of public insight into these matters. Witness the disquiet during the antiwar disputes of the early seventies about the possible softening of American youth; it was speculated this was due to their having been reared according to the ideas of Dr. Spock. And witness the growing realization of women, influenced by the writings of feminists like Germaine Greer and Gloria

Steinem (and by the debates over the Equal Rights Amendment), that their education has been grounded on questionable and outmoded assumptions. Nevertheless, the bases of popular child-rearing practices, and of deep-seated attitudes towards children, pass largely unexamined. With respect to these issues, most of us are happy to lead the unexamined life, and to tolerate ambiguity and downright contradiction. Consider the strange and conflicting beliefs that lie behind the following: a young person in the United States is judged sufficiently mature to drive a car at fifteen or sixteen, but not mature enough to vote until eighteen; in some states, a youngster can marry as early as fourteen (with parental consent), join an armed service and perhaps die for the country at eighteen, but not buy alcohol until twenty-one.

The present work has arisen from the conviction that it is unsatisfactory to leave important beliefs and practices unexamined. We bring the skills of the historian and the philosopher to bear; we share an interest in the history of ideas and have something of an international perspective (gained while teaching and researching in the United States, Australia, New Zealand, Great Britain, China, the USSR, and Papua New Guinea). Finally, we have children, have taught in schools, and have trained teachers and educational researchers.

Theories or models of children are developed, written down and published, read and discussed, dissected by academic experts, understood or misunderstood; some are influential in the research community, others are adopted by popularizers, and many are forgotten. Sometimes, by a quirk of fate, the original theories are even forgotten by the very people who were most decisively influenced by them. The historian and philosopher together can trace the development and influence of these theories, help clarify the central notions of each, and throw light on some of the misunderstandings that have followed efforts to adopt them.

In the following chapters, no attempt has been made to be encyclopedic. Rather, attention has been focused upon a small number of models of the child that have been of undoubted influence in Western thought during the last three hundred years, and that are still with us. The first chapter highlights our general approach to analyzing the models, and the remaining chapters discuss them in roughly the chronological order of the appearance of their classic formulation. As the discussion in the book attempts to mirror something of the dynamic character of Western thought, there is a degree of cross-reference throughout, and some people will be discussed in more than one context. A significant time span is covered in most chapters.

In preparing this book, we are indebted to almost a decade of students of child development and education (some of whom were also young parents) at Stanford University, who were presented with the material in their classes. While seeming to enjoy it, they were lavish with suggestions. We also owe a great debt to the staff of Melbourne University Press and, especially, to Professor R. J. W. Selleck of Monash University, who made it possible for us to publish *From Locke to Spock*, the precursor that has grown and matured into the present volume. Valerie Phillips provided vital word-processing skills, together with comments from the perspective of a concerned and interested reader.

Man is a model exposed to the view of different artists; every one surveys it from some point of view, no one from every point.

HELVÉTIUS

1.

ON SEEING CHILDREN
THROUGHOUT HISTORY

IN one of his short stories, the humorist James Thurber described the difficulties he had experienced at college in biology class. Try as he might, he was unable to see cells through a microscope. But he could focus on spots, streaks, blurs, and occasionally the reflection of his eyeball. Perhaps there were only spots, streaks, and blurs in front of Thurber the student. However, it is equally likely that these motley shapes actually constituted the cell he was seeking. He was unable to see them as a cell in much the same way that some people cannot see two faces in the well-known optical illusion of the ambiguous drawing of a candlestick.

One of several reasons why patterns of light may not be seen as a cell is that the observer may lack sufficient knowledge. Seeing shapes as a cell is a theory-laden activity; "knowledge is there in the seeing."[1] The point is, in order to see a cell through a microscope, it is necessary to have some acquaintance with modern biological theory; a person from a nonscientific culture would have little success, for he or she would not even know what counted as a cell. This is not to suggest, however, that seeing a cell is a two-stage process: first the perception of a pattern, and then the interpretation or theoretical analysis of it as a cell.[2] There is only one process, for the knowledge "is there in the seeing."

It may be suggested that the nonscientific observer actually sees the same pattern as the biologist, but of course is not in a position to recognize it as a cell. However, there is strong evidence to indicate that the actual pattern detected by the unknowledgeable observer is different from that seen by the expert. Psychologists have carried out experiments in which, though the pattern of light on the retinas of

1

several observers was the same, they reported having seen different things, according to their differing theoretical frameworks. In other experiments, different patterns projected on the retinas of observers were reported to be identical.[3]

The following experiment is revealing. Slides were made of a number of regular playing cards, but a special slide—one showing a card with the traditional color reversed (such as a black six of hearts)—was included in the set. When each slide was projected onto a screen for a fraction of a second, viewers correctly identified all except the "doctored" one—typically it was seen as blurred, but sometimes as brown or as a six of spades. The slide had to be left on the screen much longer than the others to be identified correctly. This experiment illustrates that what a viewer sees—the blur—is determined, not just by the "real" contents of the slide, but by the interaction of what is on the slide with what ideas or knowledge or preconceptions the viewer possesses. This is what was meant by "knowledge is there in the seeing." The viewer knows that a six of hearts is red, and, unconsciously, this knowledge seems to act like a filter, hampering the identification of the black playing card. The background knowledge and the incoming visual stimulus seem to interact, with the result that the viewer is conscious of seeing a blur.

Cases like this have led to the conclusion neatly expressed by Johnson Abercrombie:

> All of these examples which show that different observers, or the same observer at different times, may get different information from a picture, illustrate how the observer "projects" on to the picture, i.e., contributes ideas or imaginings of his own.[4]

And, of course, this happens not only with pictures or images in a microscope. Observation in everyday life is not exempt—what is seen is a function of the state of knowledge of the observer. All of us have undergone, from infancy, what has been called a "prolonged apprenticeship in seeing,"[5] so that we are no longer aware of exercising a skill or making use of a background of theoretical knowledge when we distinguish between the everyday objects with which we come into contact. We have come to possess what R. L. Gregory has termed "the intelligent eye."[6]

Children are among the "everyday objects" that we observe. And if the foregoing line of argument is valid, what is seen when we look at children is then, in part, a result of theories that are held and

assumptions that are made. Just as the nineteenth-century astrono-
mers Herschel and Ross saw different things when they first came
across the same spiral nebula in the heavens—one saw several con-
centric circles and the other saw a spiral—so different observers may
see different things when looking at a child, although the images on
their retinas may be the same.

§   §   §

A FASCINATING but controversial body of evidence supporting this
general thesis of the "theory-laden" nature of perception is provided
by works of art. In his famous painting of children's games, Brueghel
the Elder depicted his subjects as small adults—his children had the
same appearance, the same bodily proportions as adults, but were
simply scaled down in size, contrary to a modern understanding of
their relative proportions. A similar phenomenon can be seen in medieval paintings of the Nativity, where the infant Jesus seems gro-
tesquely proportioned to modern eyes. A different example is the
way children were seen by the painters and magazine illustrators of
the Victorian era: children from the slums of London were depicted
as unkempt but angelic, in marked contrast with the appearance of
children of similar background today. It is possible, of course, that
the artists of these earlier periods were merely technically incompe-
tent, but it seems more reasonable to recognize that the way they
saw and the way they depicted children were influenced by the theories about children that were current in the culture of their times.
They did not think of children as we do now, and they did not see
them in the same way. (It should be added that a complicating factor
in some of these examples is the use of the child throughout the ages
as an artistic symbol—a symbol of innocence, for example; furthermore, theological, political, and racial doctrines sometimes prescribed
how certain children had to be depicted.[7])

§   §   §

ANOTHER line of argument leading to the same general direction has
been presented by those philosophers of science who are interested
in the role played by models. It has been claimed that the theoretical
models used by physicists—such as the planetary model of the atom,
the wave and particle models of light, the particle or billiard-ball model
of the kinetic theory of gases—are more than mere psychological

devices that provide scientists with easily pictured analogs of complex physical situations. Models channel attention in certain directions; they are sources of hypotheses for investigation and thus help to open new areas of research. They suggest lines that explanations of new phenomena may follow.[8] Significantly, too, a model that opens up possibilities for inquiry in one direction may close off a scientist's mind from other possibilities; models, in other words, may help to hide phenomena.

If one physicist is working with the particle model of light while his colleague has adopted the wave model, the phenomena each investigates and the types of questions each is likely to set himself are quite different. The first may ask: What type of particles are light rays made of? What are the masses of these particles? How much pressure will they exert on any object upon which they shine? These questions are unlikely to occur to his colleague, who, under the influence of the wave model, may ask instead: What are the wavelengths of light of different colors? Can the phenomenon of interference, which can be observed with other types of waves, be detected in the case of light waves? According to the frame of reference of the first physicist, these latter questions are nonsensical.

Observers of children, whether they be parents, teachers, artists, or psychologists, have often adopted loose theoretical frameworks that play roles very similar to those of models in physical science. The case of the artist has already been mentioned; another example, which will be taken up in more detail later, is the work of A. S. Neill, late headmaster of the internationally famous progressive Summerhill School in the United Kingdom. His theoretical model incorporated the assumption that children are naturally good, and this led him to view children in certain ways and to ask certain questions that may not have occurred to an observer who adopted a rival model, such as one incorporating the doctrine of original sin. Whenever Neill saw a child who would have been regarded as sinful by the latter observer, he looked for factors that could have interfered with the child's natural impulses, for in his view a child was never born bad but was only spoiled by what had been undergone during upbringing. Similarly, Neill saw sickness and unhappiness where many would see only a normal or unexceptional child:

> The moulded, conditioned, disciplined, repressed child—the unfree child, whose name is Legion, lives in every corner of the world. He lives in our town just across the street. He sits at a dull desk in a dull school; and later, he sits at a duller desk in an

office or on a factory bench. He is docile, prone to obey authority, fearful of criticism, and almost fanatical in his desire to be normal, conventional and correct. He accepts what he has been taught almost without question; and he hands down all his complexes and fears and frustrations to his children.[9]

Another notion from recent philosophy of science leads the argument in the same direction. The historian of science Thomas S. Kuhn has argued that scientists normally work within a theoretical framework or paradigm. It is the paradigm of a group of scientists that determines the problems that will be selected for study, the way those problems will be conceptualized, and the techniques that will be used in their investigation. The paradigm, in other words, shapes the scientists' awareness, it focuses their attention—in much the same way that models do. Kuhn wrote that in choosing the term "paradigm" he wanted

> to suggest that some accepted examples of actual scientific practice—examples which include law, theory, application, and instrumentation together—provide models from which spring particular coherent traditions of scientific research. . . . The study of paradigms . . . is what mainly prepares the student for membership in the particular scientific community within which he will later practice.[10]

Examples of paradigms are Ptolemaic and Copernican astronomies, Aristotelian and Newtonian dynamics, and wave optics. Although Kuhn doubted whether any framework in the social sciences is pervasive enough in its influence to warrant being called a paradigm, Freudian psychology would seem to possess many of the features he discussed. Freudians tend to have the same general perspective on the world: they have common methods, they speak the same theoretical language, and they regard the same things as problems.

In any age, most scientific activity is directed at solving puzzles within a particular paradigm, but occasionally a difficulty will arise that leads to the formulation of a new paradigm that replaces the older one after a period of struggle. This is a scientific revolution.

Kuhn's theses have been controversial. He has been attacked for oversimplifying the history of science and for using the key term "paradigm" in a vague, if not ambiguous, way.[11] (Is a paradigm a general theory? A set of methods? An exemplary and trend-setting piece of work by someone of the stature of a Newton or a Freud?)

He has also been charged with opening the doors of science to relativism. The point is that Kuhn makes the selection between rival paradigms or frameworks a process akin to political conversion rather than a matter of rationally weighing up alternatives. In his view it cannot be said that one paradigm is better than another—paradigms cannot be compared in this way for they focus differently on different issues and thus are technically "incommensurable."[12] (Thus, a Freudian and a behaviorist psychologist have difficulty in rationally settling their differences, because their frameworks are so fundamentally dissimilar.)

Nevertheless, Kuhn's work has had tremendous suggestive or heuristic power, and it is particularly revealing to apply his ideas to the way children have been observed and written about through the ages. It becomes evident that there have been many paradigms or theoretical frameworks (to use Kuhn's notions loosely) that have shaped the way children were seen and treated; and generally speaking the members of a given social group, at any one period, have been inducted into the same paradigm or paradigms, although this is not to say there has always been unanimity of opinion. Certainly, too, there have been revolutionary periods when paradigms changed, and when adherents of rival paradigms had difficulty in understanding or communicating with each other.

§   §   §

AN interesting example of an important paradigm shift concerning children has been discussed by Philippe Aries in *Centuries of Childhood*. Using historical evidence drawn from art and literature, from personal diaries and memoirs, from inscriptions and statues on family tombs, and from clothing and toys of different periods, Aries examined the place of children in family life and society in France from the late Middle Ages to the eighteenth century. He reached the startling conclusion that in medieval France childhood was not seen as a stage distinct from adulthood—children simply were small adults:

> In medieval society the idea of childhood did not exist; this is not to suggest that children were neglected, forsaken or despised. The idea of childhood is not to be confused with affection for children: it corresponds to an awareness of the particular nature of childhood, that particular nature which distinguishes the child from the adult, even the young adult. In medieval society this awareness was lacking. That is why, as soon as the child could

live without the constant solicitude of his mother, his nanny or his cradle-rocker, he belonged to adult society.[13]

During the sixteenth and seventeenth centuries, Aries argued, a new framework developed, and the awareness of a distinctive stage of "childhood" gradually emerged. At first this took place among "women whose task it was to look after children—mothers and nannies," but the attitude slowly infiltrated the family circle, where it was joined by another set of attitudes that had arisen among the clergy:

> They too had become alive to the formerly neglected phenomenon of childhood, but they were unwilling to regard children as charming toys, for they saw them as fragile creatures of God who needed to be both safeguarded and reformed.[14]

As this revolutionary "paradigm" spread—as children began to be perceived as different from adults—children began to be treated differently. New customs and institutions evolved: children's games, clothes distinctive of various stages of childhood, and institutions especially designed for children's education—schools.

The work of Aries has itself been challenged, and rival accounts of how children were treated throughout history have been advanced. In other words, historians of childhood have disagreed about their own paradigms—about how they should approach their discipline— and as a result they have painted varying pictures of the views that people of past ages held about children. (If this seems unnecessarily complicated, consolation may be drawn from the fact that experts now seem to agree that as knowledge expands in the human and social sciences, matters that were apparently simple become more complex and muddled! Scholarship raises questions, but rarely answers many.) To cite one rival of Aries, the "psycho-historian" Lloyd de Mause has argued that the further one looks back in history, the bleaker the life of children becomes. The historical record is one of unremitting horror: children were beaten, starved, sexually abused, and terrorized. De Mause wrote that "the history of childhood is a nightmare from which we have just begun to awaken."[15] In de Mause's view, improvement has come about because each generation of children has been raised marginally better than the preceding one, and each in turn, on becoming parents, has done a slightly better job at raising its own offspring. And so it has gone throughout the ages—

a slow, painstaking, and "bootstrapping" movement away from bestiality.

The moral of all this for observers of children in the late twentieth century, be they parents or teachers or researchers, is that conceptions of children have changed during the course of history. Indeed, the views we have at present, and that we take for granted—the differences between children and adults, the structure of the family and its central role in child rearing, and so forth—may all have developed relatively recently. Furthermore, our present views are unlikely to endure forever. In the last few years these possibilities have been discussed in a number of books whose titles dramatically suggest the passing of our present paradigms of children—for instance, Postman's *The Disappearance of Childhood*, Suransky's *The Erosion of Childhood*, and Sommerville's *The Rise and Fall of Childhood*. Postman points to the role of the mass media in breaking down the barriers that used to exist between child and adult; children now see, and think about, things previously restricted to adults. Postman writes of the "merging of the taste and style of children and adults," and he cites figures about "alcoholism, drug use, sexual activity, crime, etc., that imply a fading distinction between childhood and adulthood."[16] On the other hand, Suransky examines what she calls the "childcare industry," with its "structural rigidity." In many day-care centers,

> the child becomes objectified because it is not the human development of the child that is fostered, but rather, how many children can be contained within the structure for the greatest amount of money and smallest number of staff.[17]

The child's play, the child's time, the child's explorations and social interactions are all controlled—manipulated for the convenience of the institutions concerned. Childhood is being eroded. Yet another diagnosis is found in Sommerville. He is concerned with the declining birthrate and the general lack of interest in children in Western societies (themes that Germaine Greer also discusses in *Sex and Destiny*). Sommerville comments that

> despite our many expressions of concern for children, experts have indicated that the interaction between parents and children has been declining for at least 20 years. There are unmistakable signs that children of all classes are suffering from neglect in American society.[18]

These are sobering analyses, and although they differ, they share the insight that, for whatever reason, our present patterns of belief are undergoing change. Thus these authors underline the fact that in a fundamental way we are no different from our ancestors—we are influenced as much by paradigms or theoretical frameworks or models, and by the values of society, as were the adults of yesteryear.

§   §   §

INTERESTING light is shed on the Western world's massive literature about children if it is viewed from the theoretical perspective just outlined: the theory-laden nature of observation, the suggestive or directive function of models and paradigms, and the possibility of paradigm change and intellectual revolution. The writings of Locke, Rousseau, Freud, Watson, Skinner, and others are revealed as major frameworks—if not paradigms—that still have an influence in the contemporary world. Each focused attention on facets of childhood that had been relatively neglected; children were seen in new ways, and as a result, new modes of treatment evolved. In the following chapters, we will be developing this argument.

Before proceeding, however, there is another matter that our theoretical perspective can help illuminate. It is an aspect of the history of childhood that has horrified many modern writers, namely, the treatment of girls. In many societies the education of girls was not given serious attention. This is reflected in books such as William Boyd's The History of Western Education,[19] where only a few paragraphs (in more than four hundred and fifty pages) were taken to summarize the views that were held about their education. This disregard for girls in turn reflected the fact that, as one historian of women put it, "the social history of women is the record of human imbecilities and errors,"[20] a phenomenon he naively traced back to simple ignorance of biological facts:

> If Adam and Eve had known some things, it would have altered their children's whole history; if St. Paul, Tertullian, Milton, Hannah More, had known some things, they would not have made the appalling mistakes with regard to women which have made them ridiculous in the eyes of all honest and just people.[21]

In recent years many scholars have joined the debate and have pointed to the economic and political advantages that accrue to men in positions of control in a society when women remain relatively powerless.

It was not only ignorance or the force of male domination that led to women and girls being treated in these unfortunate ways. How they were perceived in any era reflected the paradigms, the sets of theories or beliefs or assumptions, that were current. Given these assumptions, and given their strong directive influence on observation, theorizing, and practical life, it would have been difficult for more enlightened views to have been widely held in certain historical periods. For instance, most Athenians of the fourth century B.C. regarded women as fit only for subservient roles in society. In *The Republic* by Plato, however, an alternative paradigm was developed. Influenced by at least three sets of factors, and of course through the force of his own native genius, Plato came to look at women in a new way. First, there had been some discussion in Plato's society of the place of women, so the matter had been brought to his notice. Second, Plato was consciously attempting to rethink answers to social problems in a way that would avoid unnecessary assumptions and biases— he was, in *The Republic*, using the technique of Socratic dialogue. And third, he was extremely impressed by aspects of Spartan society, and Sparta had evolved unusually, in that women were accorded equality with men in some facets of life. As a result, Plato came to write the following dialogue between Socrates and a young Athenian, Glaucon:

> "Then if men or women as a class appear to be qualified for different occupations," I said, "we shall assign them different occupations accordingly; but if the only difference apparent between them is that the female bears and the male begets, we shall not admit that this is a difference relevant for our purpose, but shall still maintain that our male and female guardians ought to follow the same occupations."
> "And rightly so," he agreed.

After a little more argument, this conclusion was reached:

> "There is therefore no function in society which is peculiar to woman as woman or man as man; natural abilities are similarly distributed in each sex, and it is natural for women to share all occupations with men, though in all women will be the weaker partners."
> "Agreed."
> "Are we therefore to confine all occupations to men only?"
> "How can we?"[22]

Plato is a powerful figure in Western intellectual history, but even he was not able to shake popular opinion on this topic. In later ages even men who held otherwise radical ideas continued to look at women in a way that reflected traditional (if not chauvinistic) assumptions. Perhaps the most notorious example is Rousseau, for the naturalistic and revolutionary paradigm he developed for boys seemed to promise something better for girls than the position he actually endorsed:

> A woman's education must therefore be planned in relation to man. To be pleasing in his sight, to win his respect and love, to train him in childhood, to tend him in manhood, to counsel and console, to make his life pleasant and happy, these are the duties of woman for all time, and this is what she should be taught while she is young.[23]

It is, perhaps, unreasonable to expect a man who had made pioneering steps in one important direction to overthrow other paradigms of his society. Rousseau's failure is understandable: he was in many ways a creature of his times. He looked at contemporary women (who, of course, were acting in socially conditioned ways) through a network of assumptions that he had acquired from contemporary society, and it is sad, but not surprising, that he saw nothing revolutionary.

A similar argument needs to be advanced in support of a figure nearer our own day. Sigmund Freud is often criticized harshly by supporters of the women's liberation movement. His theory of women's sexuality is referred to as "this incredible invention"; he had a "patronizing and fearful attitude toward women"; he did not base his theory "upon a study of woman's anatomy, but rather upon his assumptions of woman as an inferior appendage to man";[24] and Germaine Greer has judged that "the best approach to Freud's assumptions about women is probably the one adopted by Dr. Ian Suttie, that of psychoanalyzing Freud himself."[25]

The situation is not quite so grim if approached in terms of theory-laden observation and the directive influence of paradigms. As will be discussed more fully later, Freud at first accepted various views about sex, childhood, and women that were current in the contemporary Europe of his day. It was only by degrees that he came to develop paradigms of his own. His interest became focused on certain cases he had met in clinical situations, and in response to these, he followed clues about the importance of both childhood and sex that he gleaned from his observations. His ideas were, of course, shocking to many of his contemporaries; his early collaborator broke off the relationship when he realized the direction Freud's inquiries were taking. Freud had a difficult struggle even to present his new paradigm; he can no more be blamed for failing to emancipate himself completely from contemporary society than can other scientists. His work may have had shortcomings or even have been completely mistaken, but historically it would seem that, at some personal cost, he helped produce a later climate in which a book with a title like *The Female Eunuch* could be published. At least one feminist, Shulamith Firestone, realized something of this, for she acknowledged the general pertinence of Freud's position: "He grasped the crucial problem of modern life: sexuality." But she also noted that

> Freud, in the tradition of "pure" science, observed psychological structures without ever questioning their social context. Given his own psychic structure and cultural prejudices . . . he can hardly have been expected to make such an examination part of his life work. . . . But whether or not we can blame Freud personally, his failure to question society itself was responsible for massive confusion in the disciplines that grew up around this theory.[26]

It is not an individual's acceptance of the theories, outlooks, and assumptions of his or her times—and the subsequent selective observation—that requires explanation, for this is the norm. Puzzling, rather, is why he or she came to develop a new paradigm. In the following chapters, we will investigate this and related questions with respect to key figures from the history of the development of modern views of the child.

2.

THE CHILD AND THE ENVIRONMENT

IN 1969 the *Harvard Educational Review* published an article bearing the title "How Much Can We Boost IQ and Scholastic Achievement?" Its author, Professor Arthur R. Jensen, an educational psychologist at Berkeley, became the center of a bitter controversy; his work was attacked in print, and his university life disrupted by protesting students—so much so that he hired a bodyguard. In Britain, Professor H. J. Eysenck, whose thought had developed along parallel lines, entered the fray with a book entitled *Race, Intelligence, and Education*, which supported Jensen's theme. Commenting later on the hostile reception his own work had received, Eysenck argued that too often the evidence was ignored and tactics reminiscent of those of the Nazis were adopted:

> This, then, is the *trahison des clercs* of which I make complaint: that both students and their elders and betters have begun to play a child's game of goodies and baddies, in which a man's work is judged, not in terms of its scientific content, or on any rational, empirical basis, but in terms of whether it agrees with the critic's preconceptions.[1]

What was at the center of the furor? Jensen's original essay was a detailed and technical account focusing on intelligence and scholastic achievement. He set out to discover why the programs of compensatory education that had been launched in the United States during the 1960s (as part of President Johnson's "Great Society") had generally failed to "remedy the educational lag of disadvantaged children"[2] from poor socioeconomic backgrounds and from racial minorities.

In discussing the assumptions underlying educational enrich-
ment programs, Jensen considered whether intelligence was determined by heredity to any significant extent, or whether the
environment of the child was of greater importance. He concluded
that, to a significant degree, the intelligence of a child (as measured
by IQ tests) was determined by genetic factors and that even quite
large environmental changes caused only small fluctuations. This led
Jensen to investigate whether or not there were genetic differences
between various racial groups in American society that might account
for the fact that attempts at enriching the environment of disadvantaged children had failed to improve levels of intellectual performance
significantly. Jensen concluded that indeed there were genetic factors
at work producing differences in average intelligence between racial
groups:

> There is an increasing realization among students of the psy-
> chology of the disadvantaged that the discrepancy in their average
> performance cannot be completely or directly attributed to dis-
> crimination or inequalities in education. It seems not unreason-
> able, in view of the fact that intelligence variation has a large
> genetic component, to hypothesize that genetic factors may play
> a part in this picture. But such an hypothesis is anathema to many
> social scientists. The preponderance of the evidence is, in my
> opinion, less consistent with a strictly environmental hypothesis
> than with a genetic hypothesis, which, of course, does not exclude
> the influence of environment or its interaction with genetic factors.[3]

It was for reaching this conclusion that Jensen and Eysenck were
bitterly attacked. Further fuel was added to the controversy when it
was discovered, in the mid-1970s, that the British psychologist Sir
Cyril Burt had faked some of his famous data on the similarity in the
intelligence of identical twins who had been brought up apart (i.e.,
in different environments); for several decades this data had been
heavily relied upon by those who supported the hereditarian position.[4]

The environmentalist model of the child that Jensen questioned
is one that has played an important role in the history of Western
educational and social thought, and it is a model that has underpinned
many hopes for the improvement of mankind and society. Apparently, the dashing of these hopes led many to be bitter about the
Jensenist position. Jensen set down what he considered to be the two
main constituents of the environmentalist model he was attacking,
namely, "the average children concept" and the "social deprivation
hypothesis." The first of these

is essentially the belief that all children, except for a rare few born with neurological defects, are basically very much alike in their mental development and capabilities, and that their apparent differences in these characteristics as manifested in school are due to rather superficial differences in children's upbringing at home, their preschool and out-of-school experiences, motivations and interests, and the educational influences of their family backgrounds. . . . If all children could be treated more alike early enough, long before they come to school, then they could all learn from the teacher's instruction at about the same pace and would all achieve at much the same level.[5]

The second, or social deprivation hypothesis, is the allied belief that children belonging to racial minorities or to economically disadvantaged groups who achieve only a low standard in school

do so mainly because they begin school lacking certain crucial experiences which are prerequisites for school learning— perceptual, attentional, and verbal skills, as well as the self-confidence, self-direction, and teacher-oriented attitudes conducive to achievement in the classroom.[6]

§   §   §

IT has been said that there are no new ideas, only variations of old ones. This could well apply to the dispute between the Jensenists and the environmentalists, for the two constituents Jensen identified and attacked in the environmentalist model of children can be traced back to thinkers of the late seventeenth and early eighteenth centuries who expounded them in influential ways.

John Locke (1632–1714), the English academic, doctor, philosopher, and political theorist, turned his attention to the problems of education while in political exile on the Continent during the 1680s. He was asked to write letters advising a cousin and her husband, Edward Clark, on the upbringing of their son. In undertaking this task Locke drew not only on his medical knowledge and wide personal experience but also on his carefully formulated philosophy, which later appeared in print as *An Essay Concerning Human Understanding* (1690). Locke was prevailed upon to publish his letters, and they came out in 1693 under the title *Some Thoughts Concerning Education*. It would be difficult to exaggerate the influence of Locke's work: the *Thoughts* had been through at least thirty-five English editions, twenty-one French editions, seven German editions, and six Italian editions by the end of the nineteenth century.[7]

The bases of Locke's position are revealed in his more theoretical work, *An Essay Concerning Human Understanding*. This opened with a strong attack on what was "an established opinion amongst some men, that there are in the understanding certain *innate principles*; some primary notions, . . . characters, as it were stamped on the mind of man; which the soul receives in its very first being, and brings into the world with it."[8]

Locke argued against this view by pointing out that if inborn ideas or principles existed, they should be recognized by all of mankind. But, as Locke pointed out, there was no universal assent: children and idiots, for example, were not aware of them. And even if some principles were universally accepted, this of itself would not prove that knowledge of them was inborn, since allowance must also be made for the effects of postnatal education.

After disposing of various other arguments for the existence of innate ideas, Locke was faced with a major problem:

> Let us suppose the mind to be, as we say, white paper void of all characters, without any ideas. How comes it to be furnished? Whence comes it by that vast store which the busy and boundless fancy of man has painted on it with an almost endless variety? Whence has it all the materials of reason and knowledge?[9]

This is a key issue for educationists. If the child comes into the world with a mind like white paper, an empty cabinet, a blank tablet, or a *tabula rasa* (Locke used all these expressions), where do the contents of the mind originate? "To this I answer, in one word," Locke wrote, "from *Experience*. In that all our knowledge is founded; and from that it ultimately derives itself."[10]

It does not follow that because he located the source of a person's ideas in experience, Locke must have been an environmentalist. It would have been possible to argue, along with Jensen and Eysenck, that people differ with respect to their native ability to profit from experience. Whether Locke was an environmentalist, then, depended upon the details of his theory that experience leads to the growth of human knowledge.

Locke distinguished two sources of experience, sensation and reflection. Sensation, or experience obtained via the sense organs, gives rise to such simple ideas as yellowness, whiteness, hotness, coldness, hardness, and sweetness. Reflection (or introspection, or "internal sensation") is the source of experience in which we perceive the operations of our own mind; it is by reflecting upon our own mental processes that we obtain such simple ideas as thinking, doubting, reasoning, and willing.

However, many of our ideas—"pink elephants" and "biological species" will suffice as examples—do not seem to have come directly from sensation or reflection. Locke proposed this solution to the problem:

> These simple ideas, the materials of all our knowledge, are suggested and furnished to the mind only by those two ways abovementioned, viz. sensation and reflection. When the understanding is once stored with these simple ideas, it has the power to repeat, compare, and unite them, even to an almost infinite variety, and so can make at pleasure new complex ideas.[11]

Locke's model can be pictured quite simply, as shown in Figure 1.

Once again Locke's philosophy was compatible with both the hereditarian and the environmentalist positions. The crucial issue is to what extent the child's susceptibility to sensation and reflection is determined by heredity, and to what extent the "mental powers" of combining simple ideas, contrasting them, and so on, are also thus determined.

Although not always consistent, Locke made several forceful statements that many have interpreted as setting him firmly in the environmentalist camp. The opening lines of *Some Thoughts Concerning Education* were clear enough: "I think I may say that of all the men we meet with, nine parts of ten are what they are, good or evil, useful or not, by their education. 'Tis that which makes the great difference

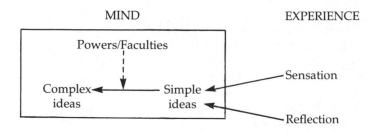

Figure 1

in mankind."[12] The nine-to-one ratio for environment over heredity is in striking contrast with Jensen's statistical and genetical calculation of a two-to-eight ratio in the other direction.

However, it would be simplistic to leave the discussion here, for another factor greatly softens the contrast between Locke and Jensen. Jensen's work focused on intelligence, whereas Locke, at least in the passage quoted above, was referring to the "moral" and "practical" traits of an individual. Jensen might well agree with Locke that environment is a much more important factor than heredity in determining whether a person is good or evil, useful or not; on the other hand, there is a possibility that Locke could have agreed with Jensen that heredity is a more potent factor in determining intelligence or the "nature of the understanding." Locke's position was not clear on this latter issue. He believed that people differed little with respect to the simple, clear ideas they had obtained via sensation and reflection;[13] he regarded the reception of these ideas as a passive process that was comparable in all mentally unimpaired people. Thus individual differences must arise from differences in the ability to produce complex ideas and to use language.[14] Locke was not prepared to commit himself on the origin of these inequalities:

> There is a difference of degree in men's understandings, apprehensions, and reasonings, to so great a latitude, that one may, without doing injury to mankind, affirm that there is a greater distance between some men and others in this respect, than between some men and some beasts. But how this comes about is a speculation, though of great consequence.[15]

§   §   §

MANY who read Locke during the following century were not so circumspect, excited as they were by the new vistas they saw under the influence of the positive aspects of the Lockean model. Children start life with the same potentialities; all inequalities between adults were due to deficiencies in, or differences between, the environments in which they were reared. In other words, both of the environmentalist theses later identified and critically assessed by Jensen were endorsed. Continental writers were particularly forthright on these matters. In his *Treatise on the Sensations* (1754), Etienne Bonnot de Condillac hit upon a striking illustration:

> We imagined a statue constructed internally like ourselves, and animated by a mind which as yet had no ideas of any kind. We

supposed the marble exterior of the statue to prevent the use of its senses, and we reserved to ourselves the right to open them at will to the different impressions of which they are susceptible.[16]

Initially, when the statue was devoid of senses, it had no ideas and no mental powers. It acquired these as it acquired the five senses. Condillac reached the conclusion that the "statue is therefore nothing but the sum of all it has acquired. May not this be the same with man?"[17]

However, it was with Claude Adrien Helvétius (1715–1771) that the environmentalist interpretation of Locke was fully developed. Helvétius had a problem similar to that of Jensen and Eysenck; the view he was advancing was unpopular at the time. So Helvétius decided that discretion was the better part of valor: "Had I published this book in my life-time, I should, in all probability, have exposed myself to persecution, without the prospect of any personal advantage."[18] He decided to "defer the publication of the work, till its author be no more."[19] The point is that a form of the hereditarian view was held by powerful groups in Western societies until quite recently, when the "wheel turned" and environmentalism became politically dominant. Those who challenged hereditarianism, from Helvétius to George Bernard Shaw (*Pygmalion* put forward an environmentalist view in which a Cockney flower-seller became as refined as a princess), could expect as hostile a reception as do those who now challenge the current environmentalist orthodoxy. Helvétius clearly recognized the danger inherent in the argument he was developing:

> If it be true that the talents and the virtues of a people determine their power and their happiness, no questions can be more important than this: are the talents and virtues of each individual, the effect of his organization, or of the education he receives?
>
> I am of the latter opinion. . . . If I can demonstrate that man is, in fact, nothing more than the product of his education, I shall doubtless reveal an important truth to mankind. They will learn, that they have in their own hands the instrument of their greatness and their felicity, and that to be happy and powerful nothing more is requisite than to perfect the science of education.[20]

Along with its implicit challenge to the myth of "birth" and the hereditary status of the nobility, this was a direct slur on the efforts of the educational establishment of the day. Secure in the knowledge that his work would become known only posthumously, Helvétius did not mince words:

> If silliness be the common condition of mankind among polished nations, it is the effect of a contagious instruction; it is because they are educated by men of false science, and read silly books. . . . The scholastic is powerful in words, and weak in argument, therefore, what sort of men does he form? Such as are learnedly absurd and stupidly proud.[21]

However, it would be wrong to interpret Helvétius negatively, as only criticizing his contemporaries, for essentially his work was optimistic and opened the door to theorizing about the future improvement of mankind.[22]

Following Locke, Helvétius believed that people are born with empty minds, and this led him to investigate the source of subsequent human inequality. He recognized a number of relevant variables: there was the possibility of hereditable differences between individuals, and individuals had dissimilar educations; he also recognized that chance factors enriched or impoverished the experience undergone by individuals. In the end he opted for an environmentalistic hypothesis: "The education necessarily different in different men, is perhaps the cause of that inequality in understandings hitherto attributed to the unequal perfection of their organs."[23] Because it was possible for education to mold men, Helvétius laid the blame for the defects of man squarely on education.[24] If education was taken out of the hands of the Church, and if governments were reformed, then, Helvétius argued, a system could be devised that would make the most of every man—physically, morally, and intellectually. This became the environmentalists' credo: mankind was perfectible through education.

§   §   §

LOCKE'S work not only contained the embryonic form of the environmentalist notion of the *possibilities* inherent in education, it also contained suggestive elements that, when developed, indicated the *methods* that should be adopted in education. Furthermore, the Lockean model of man's mode of understanding came to suggest a physiological theory that itself inspired educationists to adopt certain methods. In short, Locke's model was a paradigm that exerted its influence in a variety of ways.

Locke's view that all simple ideas, the units from which "the furniture of the mind" was constructed, came from experience eventually led to a great emphasis being placed on the efficient use of the five senses, for although Locke had identified two sources of experience, sensation and reflection (or introspection), it seemed obvious that reflection could operate only *after* some simple ideas had been produced as a result of sensation. Education through the senses, which can be called a Lockean theme, eventually led to the demand for the training of the senses themselves.

In the course of the next two hundred years, various schemes of sensory training were devised, ranging from "Kim's Game," as described by Rudyard Kipling, to the special apparatuses and sense exercises devised for kindergarten children by Maria Montessori (1870–1952), and which, in modified form, are still part of preschool education. But even more famous than these, in its day, was the major breakthrough in the "technology of teaching" known as the object lesson. First devised by the Swiss educational reformer Johann Heinrich Pestalozzi (1746–1827), these lessons became an important part of nineteenth-century educational practice. For example, in his popular teachers' college textbook *School Work* (1886), F. J. Gladman paraphrased the central portions of Locke's *An Essay Concerning Human Understanding*, and then immediately linked it with a discussion of the object lesson:

> These lessons, if well-managed, cultivate Sense-Perception, or Observation, accustom children to express their thoughts in words, increase their available stock of words and of ideas, and by thus storing material for thinking, also prepare the way for more difficult and advanced study.[25]

The idea was straightforward. The teacher came into class armed with a carefully selected object which he held up or passed around for the pupils to inspect. As Gladman said:

> Get children to look at the object, and form ideas about its size, shape, colour, and parts. Test them by questions to see how far their idea is accurate and complete, and to exercise them in using words. Direct their observation to points they may have missed. Bring other senses to bear on the object; let the children notice its hardness, softness, elasticity, roughness, smoothness, weight, texture, the sound it emits if struck, its odour, its taste, and so on as far as is desirable. Give information at proper places, partly to clear the way, partly to give completeness. . . . The proper order is Things, —Ideas, —Words.[26]

No doubt some object lessons were stimulating, but on the whole the form tended to be strained and artificial, with many teachers conducting every lesson in exactly the same way by asking exactly the same questions no matter what object was under examination. There is a story about one nineteenth-century pedagogue who taught his class that "not being transparent" was an important characteristic of the elephant! Books containing model outlines of object lessons were published that helpfully listed the materials the teacher needed for the lesson, outlined the development of the lesson, and gave the background information that the teacher was to pass on to the pupils. Sometimes the words the teacher was to write on the blackboard were printed in italics. This passage comes from the first lesson in a textbook that was in its seventeenth printing in 1861:

Glass has been selected as the first substance to be presented to the children, because the qualities which characterize it are quite obvious to the senses. The pupils should be arranged before a black board or slate, upon which the result of their observations should be written. The utility of having the lessons presented to the eyes of the children, with the power of thus recalling attention to what has occurred, will very soon be appreciated by the instructor.

The glass should be passed round the party, to be examined by each individual.

TEACHER: What is this which I hold in my hand?

CHILDREN: A piece of glass.

TEACHER: Can you spell the word "glass"? (The teacher then writes the word "glass" upon the slate, which is thus presented to the whole class as the subject of the lesson.) You have all examined this glass; what do you observe? What can you say it is?

CHILDREN: It is bright.

TEACHER: (The teacher having written the word "qualities," writes under it—It is bright.) Take it in your hand and *feel* it.

· CHILDREN: It is cold. (Written on the board under the former quality.)

TEACHER: Feel it again and compare it with the piece of sponge that is tied to your slate, and then tell me what you perceive in the glass.

CHILDREN: It is smooth—it is hard.[27]

§   §   §

UNDERLYING the use of the object lesson was the belief that the senses could be "sharpened" or "cultivated" by practice and the adoption of systematic procedures. This notion of the improvement of mental faculties by exercise was found in Locke's writings. The mind had no inborn ideas, but it did have certain powers or faculties that, after all, would produce complex ideas from simple ones. According to Locke, the mind had the faculty of perceiving or being conscious of ideas, the faculty of retaining ideas, the faculty of discerning or distinguishing between ideas, the faculty of comparing ideas, and the faculty of composition. In *Of the Conduct of the Understanding* he wrote:

> We are born with faculties and powers capable of almost any-
> thing, such at least as would carry us further than can easily be
> imagined, but it is only the exercise of those powers which give
> us ability and skill in anything, and lead us towards perfection. . . .
> As it is in the body, so it is in the mind: practice makes it what
> it is.[28]

But Locke introduced some important limitations. He did not regard memory as improvable through exercise, and he did not think that a faculty would necessarily work efficiently if applied to material that was novel; in other words, he did not believe there was necessarily "transfer of training."

Later writers were not always so moderate. Sir William Hamilton (1788–1856) believed the mind had six powers or faculties and that the cultivation of these through exercise was preferable to the acquisition of knowledge as a goal of education. This was typical of the nineteenth-century emphasis on the disciplinary or "training" value of studies. Throughout the century there were controversies over which subjects, especially the sciences or the classics, offered better "mental training."[29] The ideal of a mind with all its faculties trained and capable of being brought to bear on any problem was nicely described by John Henry Cardinal Newman (1801–1890):

> But a university training . . . is the education which gives a man
> a clear conscious view of his own opinions and judgments, a
> truth in developing them, an eloquence in expressing them, and
> a force in urging them. It teaches him to see things as they are,
> to go right to the point, to disentangle a skein of thought, to
> detect what is sophistical, and to discard what is irrelevant. It
> prepares him to fill any post with credit, and to master any subject
> with facility. It shows him how to accommodate himself to others,
> how to throw himself into their state of mind, how to bring before
> them his own, how to influence them, how to come to an under-
> standing with them, how to bear with them. He is at home in

any society, he has common ground with every class; he knows when to speak and when to be silent.[30]

Here indeed was a person perfected through education.

The theory that the mind has a number of faculties reached its most extreme form in the work of the phrenologists. Originating with Franz Joseph Gall and Johann Kaspar Spurzheim, phrenology was expounded in print for the first time in 1808. The faculties of the mind—eventually about forty were identified—were regarded not as powers but as building blocks; in other words, the mind was a composite of units or faculties. These faculties were localized in particular sites in the brain, and the state of development of each faculty could be determined by anatomical investigation because a highly developed faculty produced a swelling that resulted in a bump on the surface of the skull.[31]

In 1842 the young Herbert Spencer, shortly to embark on a career as philosopher, essayist, and unifier of science, had his head read and was told, "Such a head as this ought to be in the Church." The phrenologist's results were as follows:[32]

Alimentativeness	Moderate
Gustativeness	Ditto
Acquisitiveness	Ditto
Secretiveness	Ditto
Destructiveness	Ditto
Combativeness	Rather full
Fear	Moderate
Firmness	Very large
Amativeness	Moderate
Philoprogenitiveness	Ditto
Inhabitativeness	Large
Adhesiveness	Ditto
Love of approbation	Ditto
Self-esteem	Very large
Benevolence	Large
Marvellousness	Ditto
Hope	Moderate
Retrospect	Ditto
Conscientiousness	Very large
Veneration	Large
Identity	Moderate
Weight	Large

Colour	Ditto
Tune (Melody)	Rather full
(Harmony)	Moderate
Form	Large
Size	Ditto
Order	Ditto
Number	Rather full
Individuality	Moderate
Time	Large
Locality	Ditto
Imitation	Moderate
Constructiveness	Large
Concentrativeness	Ditto
Causality	Rather full
Comparison	Ditto
Wit	Moderate
Eventuality	Large
Language	Rather full

Not everybody, of course, subscribed to the doctrines of the phrenologists; but throughout the nineteenth century the notions of faculties and the efficacy of practice remained extremely popular, especially when stated in terms of "formal discipline" and "transfer of training."[33]

§   §   §

RESEARCH in the twentieth century has led to the downfall of some of these Lockean and post-Lockean doctrines. There has been intensive work on intelligence and the factors influencing various types of ability, on learning, and on the psychology and physiology of sense perception. A model put forward at the end of the seventeenth century could not be expected to stand unshaken in the last decades of the twentieth.

Nevertheless, many contemporary movements in education and child care continue to share Locke's general orientation. Modern kindergarten movements emphasize play, experience, and the use of the senses; many writers support mental discipline as an aim in education, but not always in the form of the narrow nineteenth-century theory of formal discipline; and there are environmentalists who support such diverse programs as compensatory education and deschooling, and who attack hereditarians like Jensen and Eysenck. Even the well-known television program "Sesame Street" is based on Lockean assumptions—its aim has been to give underprivileged children, especially in the inner cities, the simple ideas and basic experiences that their environment normally does not provide. The authors of one study of "Sesame Street's" effectiveness wrote—in a passage reminiscent of Helvétius—that at the time the program was developed,

> education was considered to be one of the more potent means of breaking out of the poverty cycle. This cycle was believed to operate by providing poorer children with few educational opportunities, thereby preventing them from securing good jobs, keeping them poor, and subsequently not allowing them to provide the educational opportunities that would help their children get good jobs.[34]

In some ways Locke was in a stronger position than his twentieth-century environmentalist descendants. His belief in the importance of education was based on a fairly simple and clear model of the way in which the human understanding developed under the influence of experience, and it was aspects of this model that proved so stimulating to thinkers of the eighteenth and nineteenth centuries. But although environmentalists of the twentieth century now have much more detailed information concerning the influence on the individual of a number of specific aspects of the environment, a clear unifying model appears to be lacking. Eysenck put the point strongly:

> It is not clear why environmentalists have failed to put their hypotheses forward in as explicit a manner as possible, make apparent the deductions which could be made from these hypotheses, and then test these deductions experimentally. If they had followed this line of work, which is clearly in accord with scientific practice, we would now know far more about the effects of the environment than we do in fact know.[35]

Eysenck argued that many people have adopted the environmentalist view because it raised the possibility of social improvement, whereas the hereditarian position seemed to imply "therapeutic nihilism." Eysenck denied this and asserted that our therapeutic or reforming activities are not limited by the facts of genetics but only by our ignorance. What is needed is further research and a frank acceptance of the facts. And in what was in effect a comment on one of the two main environmentalist theses that have formed the subject of this chapter, he wrote:

> Educationalists have always shown to an extreme degree the besetting sin of many people who wish to change the world: the refusal to acknowledge the diversity of human nature. . . . We will not succeed in changing human nature by refusing to recognize facts.[36]

But the facts are not all in, and in the meantime the Lockean model, and Eysenck's and Jensen's, live on as bitter rivals.

3.

THE FREE AND THE CONSTRAINED CHILD

THE environmentalist and hereditarian models of the child are not the only ones to have found their way into the twentieth century. An entirely different model, which highlights facets of the child to which the Lockean account paid little attention, is graphically portrayed in William Golding's best-selling novel *Lord of the Flies* (1954). The book depicts a number of English schoolboys who, on being marooned on a tropical island, descend into the stone-age barbarism of idol worship, hunting, and ritual killing. The work rejects the optimistic view of human nature shown, for example, in the nineteenth-century classic *The Coral Island* by R. M. Ballantyne. In this latter book, the castaways created a civilized paradise through plucky improvisation. Golding has been quoted as saying that *Lord of the Flies* is an attempt to trace the defects of society back to the defects of human nature. Critics noted that it expressed a position comparable to the theological doctrine of original sin—a hereditary sin incurred at conception by every human being as a result of the original sinful choice of the first man. In raising the issue of the sinfulness of childhood, Golding's critics were looking back to an important Christian tradition that over the ages has given support to practices of restriction and repression in education and upbringing, generally.

Educators in the Puritan evangelical tradition of the seventeenth and eighteenth centuries in Britain and the United States accepted that man's inherent sinfulness must be taken into account in any educational program. The tradition is exemplified in the writings of Susanna Wesley and her son John, founder of the Methodist movement. In a letter to John in 1732, Susanna set out the principal rules by which she had attempted to raise her numerous children—her son had asked for an account of her educational precepts. As she saw it, the first task of upbringing was the restraint of self-will in the child. Self-will had led Adam astray, and it was at the heart of all sin and misery in the world. Heaven awaited children whose parents expunged it; Hell, those whose parents failed them. Good habits were developed under a strict regime of controlled sleeping, fasting between meals, whispered requests for food at table, regular family prayers, and the judicious application of corporal punishment.

> When turned a year old (and some before), they were taught to fear the rod, and to cry softly, by which means they escaped abundance of correction which they might otherwise have had; and that most odious noise of the crying of children was rarely heard in the house, but the family usually lived in as much quietness as if there had not been a child among them.[1]

John Wesley's ideas on education were very much an extension of his mother's:

> Break their wills betimes, begin this work before they can run alone, before they can speak plain, perhaps before they can speak at all. Whatever pains it costs, break the will, if you would not damn the child. Let a child from a year old be taught to fear the rod and to cry softly; from that age make him do as he is bid, if you whip him ten times running to effect it. If you spare the rod, you spoil the child; if you do not conquer, you ruin him. Break his will now, and his soul shall live, and he will probably bless you to all eternity.[2]

In a sermon on the education of children, Wesley argued that education must attempt to restore the rational nature of man so far as this was possible, and he listed all the interfering "spiritual diseases, which everyone that is born of woman, brings with him into the world." They included atheism, man's worship of himself, pride, love of the world, anger, guile, and a want of mercy and justice. Atheism was to be overcome by inculcating in children the idea that "God is all in all," self-will cured by teaching children to submit to the will of the parents and by breaking the will of the child, and pride quashed by making children realize "that they are . . . more foolish, and more wicked, than they can possibly conceive."[3] Love of the world could be combated by preventing children from gratifying their senses. "The desire of the eyes must not be fed by pretty playthings, glittering toys, red shoes, necklaces and ruffles." Of the other diseases, anger was assuaged by love, guile by commanding children to speak the truth, and injustice by requiring children to render all their dues. Truly affectionate parents would not allow their children

> to vex their brothers and sisters, either by word or deed. They will not allow them to hurt or give pain to any thing that has life. They will not permit them to rob birds-nests, much less to kill anything without necessity: not even snakes, which are as innocent as worms, or toads, which, not withstanding their ugliness, and the ill name they lie under, have been proved over and over, to be as harmless as flies.[4]

Wesley's views on schooling were set out in his regulations for a girls' boarding school. The girls were to be brought up "in the Fear of God: And at the utmost Distance as from Vice in general, so in particular from Idleness and Effeminacy."[5] In the prospectus, Wesley curtly warned off any fainthearts from requesting the enrollment of their children: "The children therefore of tender Parents so call'd (who are indeed offering up their Sons and Daughters unto Devils) have no Business here." The routine of each day was rigidly prescribed. The girls were to rise at four A.M.—winter and summer—and spend an hour in religious exercises followed by a period of reflection and self-examination. At five they had to attend public worship and then work at their books until breakfast. The school day ended at five P.M.; the children then retired for an hour of private prayer followed by a short walk before supper. At seven they were at public worship again and, an hour later, were put to bed, "the youngest first." Wesley believed that no child should be left unsupervised, and he allowed them no play days. "Neither do we allow any Time for play on any Day," he declared. "She that plays when she is a Child, will play when she is a Woman." The cost of all this was to be ten pounds per annum.

§   §   §

NOT every parent interpreted in a vicious and literal way the injunction that "foolishness is bound up in the heart of a child, which the rod of correction must drive out." The famous Boston minister, Cotton Mather, wrote in 1706 that he would never give a child a blow, "except in case of obstinacy; or some gross enormity." Instead, his "first chastisement" of any of his own children was to let the offender see how astonished he was "that the child could do so *base* a thing." He added that to "be chased for a while out of *my presence*, I would make to be look'd upon, as the sorest punishment in the family."[6] But while trying to avoid physical coercion, Mather was not above bringing psychological and emotional pressure to bear to shape his children:

> When the children are capable of it, I take them *alone*, one by one; and after my charges unto them, to fear God, and serve Christ, and shun sin, *I pray with them* in my study and make them the witnesses of the agonies, with which I address the Throne of Grace on their behalf.[7]

Physical and psychological coercion or repression of children, to a degree offensive to the sensibilities of many in the late twentieth century, remained common down through the nineteenth century. In Britain, both forms were institutionalized by the famous educator Dr. Thomas Arnold of Rugby (1795–1842). He discerned evil hearts in boys, recognizing that "in the nakedness of boy-nature" there could not be found "so many as even ten righteous in a whole city."[8] Faced with this "reality," the school must act as moral purifier. Arnold accepted that the world would be a better place if there was no evil, but "evil being unavoidable we are not a jail to keep it in, but a place of education where we must cast it out, to prevent its taint from spreading."

According to Arnold's paradigm, freedom and independence were dangerous to boys in that they led inevitably to the bad conduct and depravity that was natural to such a group. His biographer, Dean Stanley, explained, using the doctor's own words: "What I want to see in the school . . . and what I cannot find, is an abhorrence of evil." The very sight of boys gathered together around the great schoolhouse fire made Arnold think "that I see the Devil in the midst of them." "From first to last," Dean Stanley recorded, "this was the great subject to which all his anxiety converged." The biographer also related how the sight of evil and the endeavor to remove it were hardly ever disjoined in Arnold, and that when Arnold thought of the social evils of the country, it awakened a corresponding desire to check the thoughtless waste and selfishness of schoolboys.

With this motivation, Arnold formulated three educational principles to guide the rooting out of evil: chapel, expulsion, and corporal punishment. Arnold had no objections to corporal punishment inflicted by boys on boys (the prefects—senior boys—at Rugby were allowed to enforce discipline), but he professed the hope that a righteous minority would escape it.

> The beau ideal of school discipline with regard to young boys would seem to be this, that, whilst corporal punishment was

retained on principle as fitly answering to and marking the naturally inferior state of boyhood, and therefore as conveying no
peculiar degradation to persons in such a state, we should cherish
and encourage to the utmost all attempts made by the several
boys, as individuals, to escape from the natural punishment of
their age by rising above its naturally low tone of principle.[9]

§   §   §

ALTHOUGH the assumptions and harsh practices bound up with the
Puritan evangelical model were challenged by supporters of "the new
education" in the late nineteenth century, the old model did not
succumb completely, and—in somewhat softened form—it has come
down to the present day. The renewed vigor of religious fundamen-
talism has been one of the features of American life during the 1970s
and 1980s; indeed, the "Moral Majority" has been a political as well
as a cultural force. Books still tell parents that

> children need to know also that the reason for this lifelong need
> for guidance arises out of the fundamental fact that we are all
> fallen creatures. . . . There are urges within our children which,
> if allowed to go uncontrolled, will ultimately ruin them.[10]

The same book, *Family Life* (1976), goes on to affirm, without mincing
words, that "all children—not just certain children, *all* children—are
born delinquent."[11] Another text in the same tradition, *The Plain Truth
About Child Rearing*,[12] starts from the identical premise and adds that
tendencies towards degeneration and selfishness are inherent in mankind. The young child, it is claimed, "learns much more quickly to
do that which is pleasurable, that which satisfies the downward pull
of his nature." As the child grows older "he or she learns many dirty
jokes in school, is exposed to the theory of evolution, hears curse words,
erotic sayings, and many other things that appeal to his human nature."
Nonetheless, man's basic nature can be contained through early training. In taking this stand, parents must reject arguments that children
pass through such stages as egocentricity or group-mindedness, for
the truth is "that at all ages children can be trained to be lovable,
obedient, helpful, self-reliant, respectful toward authority. A child
who is taught obedience from infancy will have practically no chance
of becoming a juvenile delinquent."

Good habits can be impressed and bad ones broken in a variety
of ways. Thumb sucking can be overcome by encasing the child in a

zipper-type sheet at night; a disobedient child may be put in an iso-lated place for punishment, or deprived of his favorite food; and corporal punishment can be used freely. "Any and *every* child *needs* spanking." To stop baby crying in the crib, point your finger at him and say *no*. If he continues, swat him with one or two fingers on the buttocks after first testing the force of your blows on your own forearm. Spanking can ensure that a child will eat all that is put before him and that he will learn polite table manners.

> The first time a baby drops a spoon, the parent should merely say, "No" and pick it up, placing it back in his hand. The second time, repeat the command, and swat the back of the hand sharply— it won't bruise or injure. In a very short time, you will have a very small child who will not ever, unless by pure accident in a very rare instance, drop his silverware on the floor.[13]

According to this modern version of the Puritan evangelical model, honest punishment seeks to establish habits of obedience, self-control, and discipline and is the most positive and best method of child rearing. Parents should never attempt to reason with children or shame them into good behavior—correctly used, "spanking guides and controls initiative, inventiveness and self-reliance" and will instill a deep sense of respect, discipline, self-control, and a settled, orderly appreciation of loving authority. Right habits are developed when children do what they are told, play orderly games, and are not allowed to play war games or games in which they pretend they are adults or dress up in adults' clothes. A child should listen attentively to adults at all times. Like Wesley before him, the author warned about leaving children unsupervised in play: "there is never a time when a child should be left to himself." Biblical authority is quoted to justify these programs: from *Proverbs* 4:20, "My son, attend to my words," and from *Proverbs* 29:15, "The rod and reproof give wisdom; but a child left to himself bringeth his mother to shame." Most par-ents, the author insists, never realize that these injunctions have been put in the Bible "*to teach the parent* how to teach his own child." Family study of the Bible is essential.

Over the centuries, some parents within the evangelical tradition have been ambivalent about the recommended disciplinary practices. As early as the seventeenth century, the Puritan leader John Robinson observed that it was still "much contraverted, whether it be better, in the general, to bring up children under the severity of discipline, and the rod, or no."[14] In the eighteenth century, Susanna Wesley had little sympathy for those parents who favored less severe methods—the world may judge as "kind and indulgent whom I call cruel parents, who permit their children to get habits which they know must be afterwards broken."[15] And in 1814, Crispus, writing in *The Panoplist, and Missionary Magazine*, warned readers of the existence of parents who called their children

> "harmless creatures," "pretty innocents," and other fond and endearing names which *figuratively* denote the same things, such as "little doves," "harmless birds," with a thousand other equivalent appellations; and, I confess, I never hear them without trembling lest those, their unfledged offspring, should prove birds of evil omen, if not birds of prey fitted to be taken themselves at last in the snare of the fowler.[16]

§   §   §

IT is evident that the harsh evangelical model centers around the assumption that, by nature, the child is defective: "The bias [direction] of nature is set the wrong way: Education is destined to set it right."[17] Potent arguments against this, and exposition of a model that was based on the diametrically opposed metaphysical assumption, were provided in the novel *Emile* (1762) by the erratic Swiss genius Jean Jacques Rousseau. In flowing prose Rousseau set out his new paradigm, with its controversial starting point that when things are in their natural state they are good:

> God makes all things good; man meddles with them and they become evil. He forces one soil to yield the products of another, one tree to bear another's fruit. . . . he loves all that is deformed and monstrous; he will have nothing as nature made it, not even man himself, who must learn his paces like a saddlehorse, and be shaped to his master's taste like the trees in his garden.[18]

Rousseau was a romantic—in several senses of this notoriously wide term—and certainly was not a precise and analytical writer, so it is not surprising to find inconsistencies in his work. In places he implied that the child was an amoral being who would come to know good and evil with the later development of reason. But more often Rousseau pushed the view that the child was naturally good: "Let us lay it down as an incontrovertible rule that the first impulses of nature are always right; there is no original sin in the human heart, the how and why of the entrance of every vice can be traced."[19] This, of course, focuses attention on the origin of evil, for if people are born good, how does evil enter the world? There seems to be another contradiction here. Rousseau's answer was that evil was mankind's own creation; when people come together to form societies and organizations, new pressures arise (that are not found in a state of nature), and these deprave and enslave. An individual's dependence on others was a part of the total process of corruption that started in the years when the child was brought up by ignorant care givers.

Whereas the Puritan evangelical model justified restraining and disciplining the child—the child's nature being sinful and something to be overcome—Rousseau's emphasized freedom. If the child was allowed to follow its natural impulses in an unconstrained way, all would be well. In education, Rousseau claimed, "every means has been tried except one, the very one which might succeed—well-regulated liberty."[20] The only restraint children should experience is that which comes from nature itself:

> Let him early find upon his proud neck, the heavy yoke which nature has imposed upon us, the heavy yoke of necessity, under which every finite being must bow. Let him find this necessity in things, not in the caprices of man; let the curb be force, not authority.[21]

Rousseau equated this type of freedom with happiness.

To attain freedom, Rousseau held, the earliest education must be negative: "It consists, not in teaching virtue or truth, but in preserving the heart from vice and the spirit from error."[22] Given an incorrupt childhood, a youth would learn to judge the worth of experience as his own powers of reason developed. It followed as a consequence—another apparent contradiction—that his experiences must be carefully controlled by environmental manipulation until the age of eighteen or so, a task that required skill and forethought on the part of the person charged with the child's education. Everything that is shown to children, Rousseau asserted, must be carefully selected; and he spoke of the art of controlling without precepts: "Let him always think he is master when you are really master."[23]

Rousseau admired Locke, and his accounts of the influence of experience and of how children learn put Rousseau in the environmentalist camp. The mind of the child at birth was virtually a *tabula rasa*. "We are born capable of learning but knowing nothing, perceiving nothing. The mind, bound up within imperfect and half grown organs, is not even aware of its own existence. The movements and cries of the new-born child are purely reflex, without knowledge or will."[24] However, Rousseau did accept the operation of natural, innate powers, although he made little attempt to explain them.

Another aspect of his philosophy that he did not fully explain was his concept of nature. "Whatever is natural is good," "education should follow nature," and "follow your natural impulses" are Rousseauean slogans with powerful emotional impact (examples with a more contemporary flavor would be the exhortations to practice "natural childbirth" and to consume "natural foods"). But Rousseau did not explain in what sense nature was good. Many writers have pointed out that mankind has justifiably held that some aspects of nature are not good—floods, fires, disease, and famine, for example. One simply can *define* "the natural" as "the good," but this does not seem satisfactory. Furthermore, if by "nature" Rousseau means the laws of natural necessity under whose yoke "every finite being must bow," then it is difficult to understand how mankind has any alternative *but* to "follow" (or act under) these natural forces. (The laws of nature are not things that we can *choose* to follow, they are things we *must* follow.) To be told, then, that we *should* follow nature is puzzling.

Such issues are somewhat beside the point. Rousseau was a visionary, a reformer, not a careful framer of arguments. His work aroused great passions (*Emile* was ordered publicly burned by the executioner in France), and he made many converts.

§   §   §

THE reformer's educational ideas quickly attracted a band of ardent supporters in England—Rousseauphiles like Richard Edgeworth, Erasmus Darwin, Charles Lamb, William Hazlitt, Thomas Day, and Mary Wollstonecraft. Children were brought up unable to read and write and were scared by dressed-up "ghosts" tossing them in blankets to immunize them against fright, in the manner outlined in *Emile*. Adults abandoned conventional dress and moved to the countryside, introducing themselves to Spartan regimes of living to redress the coddling of civilization. Richard Edgeworth's son was two years old when his father decided to educate him according to the new system. "He had," wrote the father,

> all the virtues of a child bred in a hut of a savage, and all the knowledge of things which could well be acquired by a boy bred in civilized society. But he was not disposed to obey, and showed an invincible dislike of control. With me he was always what I wished; with others he was never anything but what he wished to be himself.[25]

When Richard junior was seven, he and his father visited Rousseau, then living in Paris. The philosopher took the boy for a long walk and commented favorably on his education, except that when the child saw a horse or carriage he exclaimed, "That is an English horse," "That is an English carriage." Rousseau told the father that "this sort of party prejudice if suffered to become a ruling motive in his mind, will lead him to a thousand evils."[26] Edgeworth claimed later that events proved Rousseau right. Looking back, the father thought his experiment a failure, due in part to errors in Rousseau's thought and in part to his own inability to thoroughly follow the dicta through. The boy was eventually sent off to a boarding school.

Edgeworth's friend Thomas Day was another who experimented with Rousseau's ideas. Day selected two female orphans, naming one—from Shrewsbury—Sabrina Sidney and the other—from a foundling hospital in London—Lucretia. Next, he transported them to Avignon so they might be educated in "simplicity, perfect innocence (to be secured by their ignorance of the French language) and attachment to himself."[27] Lucretia proved herself "invincibly stupid," and she was discarded with a small dowry which enabled her to wed a shopkeeper. Sabrina survived longer but "failed to reach his standard in the matter of fortitude, which he tested by dropping sealing wax upon her arm and by firing pistols at her petticoats."[28]

Emile alarmed many educators who accepted the rival model of the child. The reformist evangelical Hannah More, who started Sunday schools for the children of Welsh miners, put this rhetorical question to her readers in 1799: "Is it not a fundamental error to consider children as innocent beings, whose little weaknesses may perhaps want some correction, rather than as beings who bring into the world a corrupt nature and evil dispositions, which it should be the great end of education to rectify?"[29] More thought the prime duty of the educator was to make plain to children their sinful nature, despite the fact that this was a "morose, unamiable and gloomy idea."

Another who disapproved was John Wesley. Wesley had read *Emile* early in 1770 and had jotted down his reactions in his day journal:

> Sure a more consummate coxcomb never saw the sun! . . . he is a mere misanthrope; a cynic all over. So indeed is his brother-infidel, Voltaire; and wellnigh as great a coxcomb. But he hides both his doggedness and vanity a little better; whereas here it stares us in the face continually. As to his book, it is whimsical to the last degree; grounded neither upon reason nor experience.

To cite particular passages would be endless; but anyone may
observe concerning the whole, the advices which are good are
trite and common, only disguised under new expressions. And
those which are new, which are really his own, are lighter than
vanity itself. Such discoveries I always expect from those who
are too wise to believe their Bibles.[30]

§   §   §

WHILE the twentieth-century descendants of Hannah More and the
Wesleys are William Golding and the fundamentalist authors of *Family
Life* and *The Plain Truth About Child Rearing*, there is no dearth of
successors to Rousseau. The progressive educator Homer Lane learned
the value of freedom while Superintendent of Playgrounds in Detroit
in the early years of this century. He later became head of the Ford
Republic, an institution for wayward boys. He came to believe strongly
that coercion led to antisocial behavior. In 1913 Lane was invited to
England, where he set up, with the cooperation of the courts, an
institution for delinquents called "The Little Commonwealth." Lane
imposed no rules; rather, he let the inmates evolve their own standards under the "yoke of necessity." On one occasion early in the
history of the institution, a riot broke out in the dining room and the
children broke all the plates and cups. Lane did not intervene, but
allowed them to discover that at the next mealtime there was nothing
available for them to eat with![31]

Lane's Commonwealth was an influence on perhaps the most
notable figure in the Rousseauean tradition, the headmaster of Summerhill School, A. S. Neill. (It is interesting to note that Neill naively
denied having any link to Rousseau because he had not read *Emile*.)
Like Rousseau, Neill attacked the doctrine of original sin. "When we
look at an infant," he wrote, "we know there is no wickedness in
him—no more than there is wickedness in a cabbage."[32] Because most
of the British population believed either implicitly or explicitly in the
doctrine of original sin, Neill claimed, they sought to improve children, to uplift them morally, and to train them to do good. Unhappily,
this moral instruction had the opposite effect—it actually made a child
bad. "I find that when I smash the moral instruction a bad boy has
received, he becomes a good boy."[33] In the environmentalist tradition
of Locke, bad behavior was regarded as a product of misguided early
education or the lack of love, and Neill related it to the evils inherent
in society, where coercion is used to attain "anti-life" ends. Neill
shared with Rousseau the belief in noninterference, and he accepted

that there is some innate driving force within children that leads them to make wise decisions if not interfered with by adults. "My view," he wrote, "is that a child is innately wise and realistic. If left to himself without adult suggestion of any kind, he will develop as far as he is capable of developing."[34]

One way to explore Neill's notion of freedom is by considering his references to practices in his school. He held that freedom exists where children govern themselves and where they are able to learn or play at will; Summerhill became famous for its student self-government and its weekly school meeting. Given freedom, Neill expected, students will develop good habits like self-regulation, and they will acquire the concept of equal rights for adults and children. Neill also pointed out that parents, too, must believe in freedom if their children are to attain happiness. And, again, freedom was linked with human progress in Neill's assertion that there is more freedom in each generation. Neill's "un-free" child was any who was molded, conditioned, disciplined, repressed, docile, fearful of criticism, respectful of the law and religion, and who was life-disapproving and self-hating.

Neill accepted, however, that there were necessary limits to the freedom of his pupils. He rejected the license of libertarianism or the abrogation of common sense, and sexual relations between pupils were discouraged at Summerhill (for the practical reason that they might result in closure of the school by the authorities). There was no complete social freedom either, for individuals must not trespass on the rights of others. Finally, an economic limit was fixed—operation of a "free school" was an expensive business.

Neill added an important ingredient to Rousseau's framework. Freedom was good not only because it allowed the child to be natural; it also was therapeutic, enabling the child to escape repressions, hostility, and feelings of guilt. Neill, in other words, added a Freudian dimension. He saw himself as a father figure, and he accepted the need to uncover the "hidden motives" of a child's behavior. He believed that knowledge of "where babies come from" can reduce tension in children; that it is normal for children to hold fantasies of hate, which can be resolved by being made conscious; and that society is life-hating because of the repression of sexual energy in individuals. However, Neill did not accept Freud's censorious attitude toward masturbation, arguing that adolescents punished for masturbating will not become fully orgastically potent, and that restraints on its practice can lead to unhappiness, poor health, and even colds. But for all his resorting to psychoanalysis, Neill retained some skepticism on the topic—he gave up his therapeutic sessions with children as unnecessary. Freedom, he insisted, is what cures.

While many of Neill's arguments were similar to those advanced both by Rousseau and by the psychoanalytically oriented educators of the twentieth century, it is worth reflecting again on his claim that he had not been influenced by any of the great educators. This contention seems difficult to sustain, especially as influence need not always operate through the most direct channel but can permeate in more subtle ways through society. One may be a spokesman of Rousseauean naturalism in education without having read the great romantic, perhaps even without having heard of him.

§   §   §

THE implications for education of these two rival models based on opposing metaphysical assumptions—original sin and natural goodness—have been examined by Bertrand Russell, who remembered having been shown around Westminster Abbey by Dean Stanley (Dr. Arnold's biographer and favorite pupil). Stanley, who was the model for the character of the good boy Arthur in *Tom Brown's Schooldays*, was also Russell's cousin. Even so, Russell could find little to praise in the principles of England's most revered educator:

> It is pathetic to see this naturally kindly gentleman lashing himself into a mood of sadism, in which he can flog little boys without compunction, and all under the impression that he is conforming to the religion of Love. It is pathetic when we consider the deluded individual; but it is tragic when we think of the generations of cruelty that he put into the world by creating an atmosphere of abhorrence of "moral evil," which it will be remembered, includes habitual idleness in children. I shudder when I think of the wars, the tortures, the oppressions, of which upright men have been guilty, under the impression that they were righteously castigating "moral evil."[35]

Russell commented that modern psychology had demonstrated that flogging children on weekdays and preaching to them on Sundays was not an ideal technique for the production of virtue.

Russell was hardly more attracted to the romantic naturalism of Rousseau's philosophy, claiming that its first fruits were the reign of Robespierre, and later the dictatorship of Nazi Germany. Like all appeals to the heart, Russell argued, Rousseauean propositions were incapable of refutation—what would count as proof or disproof? Russell, following Locke, thought that children were born neither good nor bad, but were morally neutral beings who could be shaped to either good or evil by the influence of their environment. However, when Russell came to put his own educational ideas into practice in his school at Beacon Hill, he adopted some methods that would have appealed to Rousseau. Timetables were posted and children were free to attend or not to attend classes, manual work was encouraged, and there were no prizes or competitions. Student self-government was instituted, and the school's declared first principle was that "one should leave one's neighbor alone to follow his own interests provided that he does not interfere with or limit the liberty for others."[36]

These models of the free and the constrained (or un-free) child both have long histories and have demonstrated a capacity to survive and persuade. Variants of both exist in the contemporary world, and are still used to justify freedom or restraint in the classroom and in the nursery at home.

4.

THE CHILD AND THE SPECIES

THE late nineteenth century was a watershed in the history of Western thought, and out of the general ferment several new models of the child emerged. One key facilitating factor was the shift of interest among psychologists away from the post-Lockean tradition that had reinforced the simplistic notion that to explain children's thought patterns, all that was necessary was to trace their accumulation of sense experiences. Perhaps the main stimulus for the abandonment of the Lockean paradigm came from the dominant intellectual preoccupation of the time—the theory of evolution. Darwin's *On the Origin of Species* (1859) is often cited as being the most influential book published in the Western world, excepting the Bible, and it would have been singular had a work of this magnitude not affected theories about the nature of children.

So it is not altogether surprising that an influential model of the child developed under the influence of the strange hybrid of evolutionary biology and embryology known as the theory of racial recapitulation. In fact, embryology had a fascination of its own and seemed to merge in scientific significance with evolutionary theory. Something of this is evident in an anecdote Darwin related in the later editions of the *Origin*. The great German embryologist Karl Ernst von Baer (1792–1876) had two embryos on his shelves that he had neglected to label, and he found that he was unable to tell if they were young lizards, birds, or mammals.[1] A serious problem was raised: why was it that animals so different in their mature forms were so similar during part of their embryonic development?

A viewpoint that related this embryological puzzle to evolutionary theory, and which kept reappearing throughout the nineteenth century (one investigator has located it in the work of seventy-two writers between 1797 and 1866),[2] was that in embryonic development individuals passed through stages similar to those through which their ancestors had evolved. Thus, if mammals evolved from reptiles, and reptiles evolved from amphibians and fish, then during embryonic development a young mammal will pass through a fish, an amphibian, and then a reptile stage. Similarly, because birds and reptiles share a common early evolutionary history, in their embryonic development a bird and a reptile will pass through the same early stages; only in the later stages of development, when the embryos are retracing or paralleling the more recent and hence divergent evolutionary histories of their respective classes, will the two embryos start to differ in noticeable ways. This theory of recapitulation obviously failed to distinguish between the distinct biological processes of growth or development of the individual on the one hand and the evolution of the species on the other.

The theory of recapitulation was known to von Baer, but he had rejected it as early as 1826:

> It has been concluded by a bold generalization from a few analogies, that the higher animals run in the course of their development through the lower animal grades, and sometimes tacitly and sometimes expressly they have been supposed to make their way through all forms. We hold this to be not only untrue, but also impossible.[3]

Von Baer went on to formulate views of his own on embryonic development; in particular, he stressed that during development heterogeneous or specialized structures arose by gradual changes out of more homogeneous or general conditions.[4]

Despite von Baer's opposition, the "parallelism" or "racial recapitulation" theory lived on. Darwin himself contributed to its longevity; he seems not to have realized the force of von Baer's objections to the theory, probably because, like many of his compatriot scientists, he was able to read German only with the greatest difficulty. Thus, in the early editions of the *Origin* he gave very tentative support to the recapitulation theory, but by the later editions was rather more confident: "On the other hand it is highly probable that with many animals the embryonic or larval stages show us, more or less completely, the condition of the progenitor of the whole group in its adult state."[5]

But it is to two of Darwin's younger German contemporaries, the biologists Fritz Muller and, more particularly, Ernst Haeckel, that the chief credit must go for popularizing recapitulation, which they elevated into "the fundamental biogenetic law":

> The two series of organic development, the ontogenesis of the individual and the phylogenesis of the tribe to which it belongs, stand in the closest causal connection with each other. . . . As I have shown, *ontogenesis, or the development of the individual, is a short and quick repetition (recapitulation) of phylogenesis, or the development of the tribe to which it belongs, determined by the laws of inheritance and adaptation;* by tribe I mean the ancestors which form the chain of progenitors of the individual concerned.[6]

Put more simply, "ontogeny recapitulates phylogeny."

Recapitulation was a colorful theory, and it has proven to be highly resistant to criticism; it turns up in surprising contexts, even today. Herbert Marcuse, the philosopher of student revolt in the 1960s, made brief use of the theory; and child-care expert Dr. Benjamin Spock wrote the following striking passage, which has been read by tens of millions of parents:

> There's nothing in the world more fascinating than watching a child grow and develop. . . . Each child as he develops is retracing the whole history of mankind, physically and spiritually, step by step. A baby starts off in the womb as a single tiny cell, just the way the first living thing appeared in the ocean. Weeks later, as he lies in the amniotic fluid in the womb, he has gills like a fish. Toward the end of his first year of life, when he learns to clamber to his feet, he's celebrating that period millions of years ago when man's ancestors got up off all fours. . . . The child in the years after six . . . is probably reliving the stage of human history when our wild ancestors found it was better not to roam the forest in independent family groups but to form larger communities.[7]

§   §   §

LIKE all scientific theories that have influenced thought in fields outside the ones in which they were originally formulated, the theory of racial recapitulation had great suggestive power, especially when applied to the twin fields of child study and education. It is apparent that suggestive power is not necessarily related to validity; even an untenable theory—such as racial recapitulation—may suggest novel lines of inquiry when applied in a different field.

The work of Herbert Spencer (1820–1903) can be taken as the first illustration. The eccentric Spencer was a man of enormous energy who devoted the last forty years of his life to writing the volumes of his *System of Synthetic Philosophy*, in which he applied a conception of evolution to a variety of subjects. The manner of this conception's birth throws light on Spencer's unconventional personality. In 1840 he read a geological text that attacked the pre-Darwinian doctrines of evolution, and being "counter-suggestible" he accepted evolution immediately. His belief in the theory shows quite clearly in the numerous articles he published during the 1850s, and when Darwin's *Origin* appeared at the end of the decade, Spencer regarded it as confirming his own general beliefs.

Spencer soon incorporated the embryological ideas of von Baer into his own evolutionary framework. In 1851 he was invited to review a new edition of a physiological text:

> In the course of such perusal as was needed to give an account of its contents, I came across von Baer's formula expressing the course of development through which every plant and animal passes—the change from homogeneity to heterogeneity . . . this phrase of von Baer's expressing the law of individual development, awakened my attention to the fact that the law which holds of the ascending stages of each individual organism is also the law which holds of the ascending grades of organisms of all kinds. And it had the further advantage that it presented in brief form, a more graphic image of the transformation, and thus facilitated further thought. Important consequences eventually ensued.[8]

Clearly, Spencer was impressed with the suggestive power of von Baer's formula: the "graphic image of transformation" that it presented "facilitated further thought" and led eventually to "important consequences." Spencer's case is equally interesting in that it illustrates how little control an author has over how his or her work is used. Although von Baer rejected the theory of recapitulation, denying that individual growth paralleled evolutionary development (in fact, von Baer also opposed evolutionary theory), Spencer used von Baer's formula of growth from homogeneity to heterogeneity to formulate his own theory of parallelism or recapitulation. Above all else, Spencer was a systematizer, and he wanted to find a single principle underlying the processes that occurred in the natural world. Von Baer's embryological formula gave him what he was looking for; and if his autobiographical statement can be believed, from the start Spencer applied it not only to the growth and development of the individual, but also to the evolutionary development of species, an entirely different process. He saw individuals growing, and species evolving, along parallel paths leading from homogeneity to heterogeneity.

By 1862 Spencer was applying his evolutionary formula to a tremendous variety of phenomena: to the solar system, to organisms and species, to societies, and to "super-organic products—Language, Science, Art, and Literature."[9] He stated his formula in the following way: "Evolution is an integration of matter and concomitant dissipation of motion; during which the matter passes from an indefinite, incoherent homogeneity to a definite, coherent heterogeneity; and during which the retained motion undergoes a parallel transformation."[10] Spencer took particular offence at a Mr. Kirkman, who had parodied this formula by translating it "into plain English": "Evolution is a change from a no-howish, untalkaboutable, all-alikeness, to a somehowish and in-general-talkaboutable not-all-alikeness, by continuous somethingelseifications, and sticktogetherations."[11]

Because Spencer saw all phenomena in terms of his formula of evolution, it is not surprising that his influential educational works also bore its stamp. Spencer wrote four separate essays that were later published together in book form under the title *Essays on Education* (1861). Over the next two decades the collection was translated into fifteen languages, and by the end of the century well over fifty thousand copies had been sold in England alone—in nineteenth-century terms, a mammoth best seller.[12]

In "What Knowledge Is of Most Worth?," the first essay in the collection, Spencer divided the tasks of life into a hierarchy of categories, ranging from "those activities which directly minister to self-preservation" at one end to "those miscellaneous activities which fill up the leisure part of life" at the other.[13] This, of course, was the order of their evolutionary importance. He went on to argue that education should be "regulated" by this conception. While attention should be paid to all the tasks during the course of an individual's education, attention should be "greatest where the value is greatest; less where the value is less; least where the value is least."[14] It followed for Spencer that "science" was the knowledge of most worth.

It was not apparent to Spencer that he had fallen into an old philosophical trap by deriving an "ought" from an "is." From what he regarded as facts about nature—in this case the evolutionary priority of human activities—he concluded that it followed that education ought to have certain features. But since the time of David Hume (1711–1776) it has been realized that this conclusion is illicit. What *is* the case is an empirical matter; what *ought* to be the case is an ethical question. The point Spencer missed was made clearly by one of the founders of modern educational psychology, E. L. Thorndike, around the time of Spencer's death: "The need of education arises from the fact that what *is* is not what *ought* to be. Because we wish ourselves and others to become different from what we and they now are, we try to educate ourselves and them."[15]

Spencer's most forceful use of evolutionary and specifically recapitulationist arguments in the *Essays on Education* comes in the chapter on "Intellectual Education," where he supported teaching methods that "carry each child's mind through a process like that which the mind of humanity at large has gone through."[16] Approaching education from this direction meant presenting particulars to children before they were faced with the relevant generalizations; hence, many abstractions would not be taught to children until much later than was usually the case. For example, Spencer argued that grammar should be taught only after a particular language could be spoken; this was, he said, an "inference" that could be drawn from the relationship between the evolution of the race and the development of the individual. Education must proceed from the simple to the complex, from the indefinite to the definite, from the concrete to the abstract, and from the empirical to the rational. Spencer also noted with approval the growing desire to make the acquisition of knowledge pleasurable rather than painful. His work became immensely popular in the United States, and his ideas were taken up by the movement known as social Darwinism.[17]

§   §   §

SPENCER'S recapitulationist views of children and education, with their foundations in evolutionary biology and von Baer's embryology, reinforced the recapitulationist position that had been imported into the United States from Germany, where it had been independently developing toward its culmination in Haeckel's biogenetic law. The German version of the theory became known to educationists as the theory of cultural epochs, and it was disseminated in the latter half of the nineteenth century by Tuiskon Ziller, a disciple of the famous philosopher and psychologist Johann Friedrich Herbart (1776–1841), and by Ziller's own follower W. Rein of the University of Jena. In 1893 Rein wrote this informative outline of the history of the theory:

> We find that this idea of the analogy between the individual and general development of humanity is a common possession of the best and most noted intellects. It appears, for example, in the

works of the literary heroes Lessing, Herder, Goethe and Schiller; with the philosophers Kant, Fichte, Schelling, Hegel, Comte; with the theologians Clement of Alexandria, Augustine, Schleiermacher; with the Darwinists Huxley and Spencer; . . . with the pedagogues Rousseau, Pestalozzi, Froebel, Diesterweg, Herbart, Ziller and others.[18]

The work of Herbart and his followers was known to many of the Americans who studied in Germany in the last part of the nineteenth century, and a Herbart Club was founded in the United States in 1892. (Later this club changed its name, and as the N.S.S.E., or the National Society for the Study of Education, it is still flourishing today.) One of its members explained the theory of cultural epochs as follows:

The thought over which Ziller most loved to linger, and for which he cites a host of witnesses, is the somewhat poetic idea, which certainly has biological analogy, that each child in his development from infancy to manhood passes through the same general stages that the race has passed through in its rise from savagery to civilization. This is the argument: Just as the embryo of one of the higher animals shows unmistakeable evidence of passing through all the essential stages of development manifested by lower orders, so the child in his mental evolution passes through, in little, all the great culture epochs that have marked the development of the race.[19]

This passage suggested that there was an analogy between the development of an embryo through evolutionary stages (Haeckel's "ontogeny recapitulates phylogeny") and the growth of a child through certain cultural stages.

The cultural-epochs theory was taken seriously, and it soon appeared as a basis for school curricula. One suggestion for American schools was to coordinate the subjects taught in each grade by concentrating upon a core of cultural material; in successive years this material would draw the child along the path traveled by the race. In the first year of schooling the core material could be Grimm's fairy tales, *Robinson Crusoe*, and Bible stories from the time of the Patriarchs. Other material studied could also stem from this: for example, in science or nature study, wheat could be grown and examined at the time that Robinson Crusoe's similar agricultural adventures were being read. By the eighth year of school the child would have progressed to a cultural core consisting of Frederick the Great, the Napoleonic wars, and the restoration of the German empire.[20]

In the view of many, however, this racial progression was no mere biological analogy. Along with Spencer they saw embryonic development, child growth, and evolutionary development as actually being parts of the same process. Thus, the cultural-epochs theory soon found its way into educational journals and research programs. A typical article appeared in 1900 in the journal *Pedagogical Seminary* (which is now published under the title *Journal of Genetic Psychology*). The author claimed that during fetal existence and in the first month after birth, the human child recapitulated the invertebrate and cold-blooded vertebrate stages; during the next two months of life the earlier mammalian or ape stage was entered; during the second year of life the child repeated the evolutionary stages linking the ape to man (this was the "imperfect hand" stage of development); and in the third year the child entered the purely human stages of its growth.[21]

The editor of *Pedagogical Seminary* had no reservations about the recapitulation or cultural-epochs theory, and his journal became its acknowledged champion, printing many articles of this genre. As the journal flourished, its editor, G. Stanley Hall, found himself the leader of the American child-study movement. Hall (1846–1924) had originally intended to enter the ministry, but a year at the Union Theological Seminary led him to abandon this plan. After preaching a trial sermon, Hall had visited one of his professors for a critique; the latter was so disturbed by the content of Hall's oration that instead of discussing it, he sank to his knees to pray for Hall's soul. Hall set out for Germany where he studied a fascinating variety of subjects. Returning home, he taught English literature and philosophy, and studied psychology under William James, earning the first American Ph.D. in the subject. He capped his studies by returning to Germany to work with the noted experimental psychologist Wilhelm Wundt.

Although his variegated background illuminates Hall's subsequent work and influence, these cannot be understood apart from his devotion to Darwinism. He wrote in his autobiography: "As soon as I first heard it in my youth I think I must have been almost hypnotized by the world 'evolution,' which was music to my ear and seemed to fit my mouth better than any other."[22] And a revealing passage follows:

> In the days when my interest in child study was at its height I was once introduced to an audience by an over-zealous friend as the Darwin of the mind, and extravagant and absurd as I knew

this to be, it gave me more inner satisfaction than any compliment ever paid me by the most perfervid friend.[23]

It was Hall's passion for evolutionary theory that led him to embrace the theory of recapitulation. He believed that "infancy, childhood and youth are three bunches of keys to unlock the past history of the race," and he described psychology as the study of the "embryology of the soul."[24] Sometimes he used his evolutionary studies to throw light on child growth, as when he wrote an article on "What We Owe to the Tree-life of Our Ape-like Ancestors."[25] At other times he argued the reverse, using data concerning human growth to throw light on earlier stages of man's evolutionary history—such as when he held that the four years between the age of eight and puberty represented in

the recapitulation theory, a long period in some remote age, well above the simian, but mainly before the historic period, when our early forebears were well adjusted to their environment. . . .
In this age, which we will call the juvenile, the individual boy today is a precious key for the reconstruction of a stage in the history of the race otherwise very obscure.[26]

Everything was grist to Hall. He studied the way children make collections of objects, the variations of children's dolls, and children playing in a sandpile. He wrote a major treatise on adolescence; made a psychological study of Jesus, which, he said, earned him "odium theologicum"; and introduced Freud to the United States, which earned him "odium sexicum." Hall also wrote on "natural education" and founded and edited the *American Journal of Psychology* and *Pedagogical Seminary*.

Typical of Hall's work in the child-study movement was his influential study "The Contents of Children's Minds" (1883), in which he set out to discover the stock of experiences that children typically brought with them when they entered school. The results startled him: he discovered that 65 percent of the children reported on had not seen or had no concept of an ant, 55 percent did not realize that wooden things come from trees, and so on. Hall came to the conclusion that "there is next to nothing of pedagogic value the knowledge of which it is safe to assume at the outset of school-life,"[27] and he urged that each teacher and teacher-in-training should "explore carefully section by section children's minds with all the tact and ingenuity he can command." He closed the work by noting that the order in which children acquired concepts "varies very greatly with every change of environment."[28] In this aspect of his work he was a precursor of Piaget.

The views of Hall, Spencer, and Ziller gained wide popular currency and influenced far more than just research in child study and education. One example from literature is the work of Jack London. In his popular short novel *The Call of the Wild* (1903), London described the adventures of Buck, a magnificent dog who was stolen from his owner and sold as a sled dog in Alaska at the time of the gold rush, when good dogs were at a premium. Buck fell more and more under the spell of instincts that had been prevalent in the early stage of his canine evolutionary history, the traces of which persisted in the adult stage of modern dogs:

> And not only did he learn by experience, but instincts long dead became alive again. The domesticated generations fell from him. In vague ways he remembered back to the youth of the breed, to the time the wild dogs ranged in packs through the primeval forest and killed their meat as they ran it down.[29]

Buck's case was a literary expression of part of Hall's position, for the latter wrote of the "deep and strong cravings in the individual to revive the ancestral experiences and occupations of the race."[30] Buck's succumbing to his racial instincts in this way had something in common with the Nazis' later emphasis on "blood" and "race," which can also be traced back to an Haeckelian origin.

§   §   §

THE major educational thinker of the early twentieth century, John Dewey, could not remain uninfluenced by a theory as widespread as racial recapitulation. Dewey knew of the recapitulationist views of Ziller and Rein, as well as those of Hall. He had studied psychology and pedagogics under Hall as a doctoral student from 1882 to 1884, and later he was one of the leading figures in the Herbart Club. There are clear signs of the influence of the theory of recapitulation in Dewey's widely read *The School and Society* (1899). This book originated from talks Dewey gave about the Laboratory School that was under his control while he was a professor at the University of Chicago. Discussing the activities of seven-year-olds at the school, Dewey wrote:

> Many anthropologists have told us there are certain identities in the child's interests with those of primitive life. There is a sort of

natural recurrence of the child mind to the typical activities of primitive peoples; witness the hut which the boy likes to build in the yard, playing hunt, with bows, arrows, spears, and so on. Again the question comes: what are we to do with this interest— are we to ignore it, or just excite and draw it out? Or shall we get hold of it and direct it to something ahead, something better? Some of the work that has been planned for our seven-year-old children has the latter end in view—to utilize this interest so that it shall become a means of seeing the progress of the human race.[31]

This passage indicates that in applying the theory of recapitulation to education, Dewey tempered it somewhat, almost certainly in light of the pragmatic philosophy he was currently developing. Later, in an article published in an encyclopedia in 1911, he specifically listed qualifications that he believed had to be "introduced regarding the use of this doctrine."[32] By the time he produced his major educational work *Democracy and Education* in 1916, Dewey had rejected racial recapitulation. He recognized that the biological basis of the theory was false, and he claimed that the theory led to underestimating the directive influence of the present environment on the young.[33] But he acknowledged that the human infant did begin life as an immature being with many conflicting impulses and that it was a "part of wisdom to utilize the products of past history so far as they are of help for the future."[34]

What happened between 1911 and 1916 to cause Dewey to change his mind about recapitulation or cultural epochs was the publication in 1913 of a vigorous attack on the theory by the psychologist E. L. Thorndike. The latter had argued that the biogenetic law "ontogeny recapitulates phylogeny" was true "in only a very vague and partial way. Only in rough outlines and in the case of a fraction of bodily organs does nature make an individual from the fertilized ovum by the same series of changes which it made his species from the primitive protozoa."[35]

Thorndike played havoc with the arguments of the recapitulationists. He pointed out, for example, that if a young child had tendencies to thought or action that were characteristic of a fish or monkey or very primitive man, it would be reasonable to expect that his brain would be similar to the brain of a fish, monkey, or primitive man. This was not the case. Thorndike then turned to expose some of G. Stanley Hall's confusions; he showed that in Hall's view the newborn baby "not only 'makes paddling and swimming movements' *qua* fish, but also has a 'horror of water' *qua* monkey." Thorndike remarked that "such defences of the recapitulation theory are obviously more dangerous to it than the most violent attacks."[36] He summarized his attacks on the theory by concluding that "one cannot help thinking that the influence which it has exerted upon students of human nature is due, not to rational claims, but to its rhetorical attractiveness."[37]

Perhaps this explains why the recapitulationist view of child growth retained its appeal through the twentieth century, and why it appears in the writings of such diverse figures of the modern world as Marcuse and Spock. And it cannot be doubted that this "rhetorically attractive" theory led many people to devote themselves to the fields of child study and education, where they did valuable work. The theory thus gave the child-study movement a momentum it has not yet lost.

5.

THE LOSS OF INNOCENCE:
THE FREUDIAN CHILD

WHILE Spencer and Haeckel were going into evolutionary raptures and thereby bolstering the dominant paradigm of the late nineteenth century, a revolutionary position was being developed in Vienna. Psychoanalysis, formulated as Sigmund Freud tells us, by himself, reflected a multitude of influences: it spoke the language of the people by admitting the evidence of their myths and folklore at the same time as it accommodated facts and analogies gleaned from the humanities and the major scientific theories of the day. It also took over the important concept of the unconscious from the rich Continental philosophical tradition. But Freud's model also owed much to the state of the medical sciences of the day, although there has been a recent suggestion that this aspect of Freud's work has been systematically overemphasized by the translators of his writings.[1]

When Freud completed his medical training and went to work as a research scientist, he looked at children primarily as specimens— as subjects who could be useful in advancing his studies in the laboratory. In the early 1880s, for example, he was examining the nerve tracts of fetal brains and was using kittens, puppies, and infants to demonstrate that their embryonic tracts persisted in the complex, mature adult sections. By the end of the decade he had written papers on paralysis and *enuresis nocturna* and, in 1897, had prepared a lengthy treatise on cerebral palsies in children for an encyclopedia of medicine.

Largely for financial reasons, he was forced to give up hopes of a future in the laboratory, and he returned to clinical life and began specializing in the treatment of neuropathology. It was not long before Freud abandoned the search for a physical or neurological basis for hysteria, and with it such conventional remedies as hydro- and electro-therapy, in favor of the psychological "talking cure," which relied on the touch of a hand to the forehead and probing questioning. By 1900, Freud had thoroughly accepted a new paradigm according to which symptoms like hysteria were susceptible to treatment by ideas alone. In taking this stand he moved away from the materialistic position of the physiological school of Helmholz in which he had been trained, according to which humans were machines whose activities were explicable solely in terms of physiochemical mechanisms. In one of his later papers discussing patients' fantasies, Freud put his position clearly: "The phantasies possess *psychical* as contrasted with *material* reality, and we gradually learn to understand that *in the world of the neurosis it is the psychical reality which is the decisive kind.*"[2]

Certainly, Freud did not shed his youthful allegiances entirely. It was his alertness to the importance of biochemistry, for instance, that led him to anticipate the discovery of sex hormones. His choice of language, too, reflected his past. He likened the psychical (or psychological) attributes of civilized humans to organic substances with their traces of the chemical elements, and noted how psychoanalysis had followed the path of chemistry by relating quantitative differences with qualitative variations. Then there was his so-called hydraulic formula, whereby he attempted to explain mental processes through waves, residues, and channels. He even argued that it was theoretically possible for the psychical determinants of every detail of the processes of the mind to be known; for, still partly under Helmholz's influence, Freud remained a convinced determinist. The events of psychical life, he maintained, were just as much caused (and "non-accidental") as events in the physical world—the nature of the cause simply differed. In the third of five lectures on psychoanalysis that he gave in the United States early in the twentieth century, on G. Stanley Hall's invitation, Freud stated that

> psycho-analysts are marked by a particularly strict belief in the determination of mental life. For them there is nothing trivial, nothing arbitrary or haphazard. They expect in every case to find sufficient motives where, as a rule, no such expectation is raised. Indeed, they are prepared to find *several* motives for one and the same mental occurrence whereas what seems to be our innate craving for causality declares itself satisfied with a *single* psychical cause.[3]

The model that Freud painstakingly developed under these influences, or rather, the series of models (for there was more than one, and Freud's ideas kept developing throughout his life), broke with tradition in a number of ways. Jerome Bruner, one of the leading contemporary psychologists of the English-speaking world, and certainly no close follower of Freud's, assessed the contribution of psychoanalytic theories to modern thought as fivefold. Freud established continuities in five areas where his contemporaries and predecessors had thought there were only discontinuities: first, the continuity of lawfulness throughout nature, in both the physical realm and the realm of human thought and feeling; second, the continuity between the primitive, the archaic, and the infantile on one hand and the civilized and the evolved on the other; third, the continuity between the child and the adult; fourth, the continuity between rational and purposive waking life and the apparent irrationality and purposelessness of dream and fantasy life; and fifth, the continuity of mental illness with mental health.[4]

§   §   §

IT is customary to date the beginnings of psychoanalysis from Freud's collaboration with Dr. Joseph Breuer on the work *Studies on Hysteria* (1895). From then until 1900, "Freud developed theories of unconscious motivations, repression (the process of making an experience unconscious), resistance (the way in which it is kept unconscious), transference (the emotional relationship between analyst and patient), and the causation of the neuroses."[5] Freud's overwhelming desire to categorize, identify, and assign specific causes—as well as his conscious search for some major discovery, for the usual personal reasons—contributed to his share of theoretical false starts. Among the avowed blind alleys of Freud's early papers was the so-called seduction theory, in which he attributed hysteria in his patients to instances of sexual molestation in childhood. Later in his career he was to accept that these scenes of seduction were neurotic symptoms based on fantasies that were products of the underlying Oedipus complex—on which he had stumbled unawares. In 1897, a year after publication of the seduction theory, he admitted privately to a close friend that his hypothesis was untenable; however, the public had to wait until 1905, when Freud had the theory of infantile sexuality with which to replace it, before they learned that he now accepted that the theory had collapsed under the weight of its own improbability. By one of the twists and turns in the history of ideas, Freud's original seduction theory appears less farfetched today, given revelations of the extent of child abuse in Western homes.

Before Freud, it was commonly, although not universally, held that childhood was sexless and that manifestations of sexual curiosity by the young were signs of unnatural precocity. (It can be imagined what the attitude of the Wesleys, Cotton Mather, and Dr. Arnold was toward this phenomenon.) However, in constructing his theories about the nature and events of childhood, Freud turned to the power of the sexual as deliberately as his contemporaries had passed it by. In his *Three Essays on the Theory of Sexuality* (1905), which were subject to modification and extension over some twenty years, Freud discovered sexuality in the developing infant: the oral stage with its pleasures of sucking and being fondled gave way to an anal-sadistic period that brought mastery of the bowels and a measure of independence for the child, who now could decide whether to please his parents with his "gifts" or disobey them by withholding his feces. Along with the child's newfound power came some idea of the differentiation of self and environment. The final stages of sexuality in the years up to six was the phallic, when boys discovered their penises. Freud thus recognized "that beginnings of an organization of the sexual instinctual components can be detected in the sexual life of children from its very beginning."[6]

From about the age of six, the child entered a period of latency, which continued until puberty. Sexual urges were repressed and restrained until the socially acceptable attitudes of shame, disgust, and pity appeared that would allow the child to join in adult community life. The price of the suppression of sexuality was that the openness and charm of the nursery years disappeared and the child became less curious and intellectually duller. By tracing these preordained stages of development, Freud mapped the hitherto undiscovered world of the sex life of the young child. His new theory attacked the view that the child's sex life emerged ready-made at puberty; rather, it passed through successive stages from birth, after the fashion of a caterpillar becoming a butterfly. The course that sexuality took in infancy proved decisive in determining whether a child would remain healthy throughout life or "whether and at what point the individual shall fail to master the real problems of life."[7]

§   §   §

THE second major construct in Freud's theorizing on infantile sexuality, the Oedipus complex, was formulated in 1910. Sons, Freud claimed, sexually desired their mothers, and he compared such incestuous desire to the condition of King Oedipus, who inadvertently wed his mother after murdering his father. Although this deed of Oedipus represented the fulfillment of every boy's secret wish, its antisocial character meant that the young must be taught to renounce the temptation. The means was the threat of castration. This could follow from a mother's thoughtless warning when she became aware of her son's habit of touching his genitals, or if no direct threat was present, fear of emasculation had the power to surface spontaneously out of man's archaic heritage around the age of five or six years. Under the influence of the theory of racial recapitulation, Freud accepted that the deed of Oedipus possessed historical truth, that the sons of early man had in fact risen against their father and present man had inherited the guilt of this murder. Freud believed that the Oedipus complex was at the nucleus of every neurosis and was the basis of the unconscious mind.

A corollary of the Oedipus complex was that decisive repressions took place in early childhood. In his *Autobiography*, Freud described how he was

> carried further and further back into the patient's life and ended by reaching the first years of his childhood. What poets and students of human nature had always asserted turned out to be true: the impressions of that early period of life, though they were for the most part buried in amnesia, left ineradicable traces upon the individual's growth and in particular laid down the disposition to any nervous disorder that was to follow. But since these experiences of childhood were always concerned with sexual excitations and the reaction against them, I found myself faced with the fact of *infantile sexuality*—once again a novelty and a contradiction of one of the strongest human prejudices.[8]

Freud set limits on the extent to which infantile sexuality could be affected by cultural and social influences. He did not doubt, though, that where moral and intellectual levels were low, some neuroses were avoidable, for sexual urges might go unrestrained. This explained why hysteria was less common among the working classes. In his case study *Dora*, Freud mentioned that her constitution and cultivated upbringing predisposed her to depression; he surmised that she could have avoided illness by relieving her tensions through an abandonment to sexuality and perversion. Such relief from neurosis, though, was purchased at the cost of high culture. Freud stated the problem:

> What attitude should we adopt towards the sexual activity of early childhood? We know the responsibility we are incurring if we suppress it; but we do not venture to let it take its course without restriction. Among races at a low level of civilization, and among

the lower strata of civilized races, the sexuality of children seems to be given free rein. This probably provides a powerful protection against the subsequent development of neuroses in the individual. But does it not at the same time involve an extraordinary loss of the aptitude for cultural achievements? There is a good deal to suggest that here we are faced by a new Scylla and Charybdis.[9]

The sexual life of civilized man must be seriously impaired, for he was both the bearer and victim of his civilization. So far as the child was concerned, Freud again was preaching a theme novel for his times, that only the children of barbarians could be happy; this, of course, was the Rousseauean message, but with a new theoretical underpinning.

§   §   §

AN important avenue of access to the hidden secrets of childhood was the interpretation of dreams, which, Freud believed, could break down infantile amnesia and disclose the contents of the unconscious. Dreams were not trivial; for Freud they were psychic phenomena with as much rationale as the acts of waking life. He claimed to have learned about his own personality and childhood by this method of interpretation. The deliberately backward-looking character of this process immeasurably increased the significance of the early childhood years. Dream analysis, with its demonstrations of human egotism and incestuous love choices, further convinced Freud of the validity of infantile sexuality and of the power of the infantile in the human makeup; the various elements of his system were coalescing and becoming mutually supportive:

> A regularly formed dream stands, as it were, upon two legs, one of which is in contact with the main and current exciting cause, and the other, with some momentous event in the years of childhood. The dream sets up a connection between those two factors— the event during childhood and the event of the present day— and it endeavours to reshape the present on the model of the remote past.[10]

Each night, the child present in every adult pursued its existence afresh, and on waking, the force of the infantile lingered on in the unconscious.

However, Freud doubted whether adult dreams *directly* reflected themes from childhood. He believed that their outward form reflected other motives that would have to be recognized before the infantile source could be exposed. Dreams, in other words, had their messages disguised—they were heavily symbolic. Dream analysis was especially important for those experiences of early childhood that had not been understood at the time but were subsequently understood in adulthood. Analysis was important, too, for its revelation of the entire development of the human race, according to the racial recapitulation notion:

> The prehistory into which the dream-work leads us back is of two kinds—on the one hand, into the individual's prehistory, his childhood, and on the other, so far as each individual somehow recapitulates in an abbreviated form the entire development of the human race, into phylogenetic prehistory too.[11]

The dreams of young children, as opposed to those of adults, were important because they were generally uncomplicated, at least up to the fourth or fifth year; this made them useful for probing the unconscious and theorizing about the origins and functions of dreaming itself. Freud, in contrast with his contemporaries, saw them as intelligible and important mental acts. Most children's dreams embodied simple wish fulfillment related to some immediate experience— hence a little girl's dream about a lengthy lake crossing, following a too-short excursion of the previous day. Children dreamed of fairy tales and of legends come true, of the physical demands of hunger and thirst; and some dreams had components related to autoerotic stimulation, like wrestling and romping. Dreaming also had its own symbolism, with parents often appearing as emperors and empresses, and brothers and sisters as small animals and vermin. Such symbolism, rooted in mankind's past, possessed a universal quality.

§   §   §

As a result of these investigations, Freud concluded that the innocence of childhood was a myth based on adult wishful thinking. Thus, he achieved a new insight into childhood, arguing that the list of children's instincts that had been built up over the years by parents, teachers, doctors, and philosophers was seriously deficient as it omitted one of the most basic. Previous attitudes and assumptions would have to be changed to accommodate the fresh findings. It would now have to be accepted that in the infant years, children will demonstrate the entire gamut of sexual activity, from a desire to seduce the opposite sex to exhibitions of what appear to be perversions. Children can be homosexual, cannibalistic, libidinous, and sadistic creatures who vent adultlike emotions of rage, envy, and fear on their younger brothers and sisters. In this children are not freaks or degenerates; rather, they are following a course of child development predetermined for all.

By describing child behavior in these terms, Freud broadened the commonly accepted definition of sexuality, applying it to bodily functions not directly associated with human reproduction or adult perversion. When a child touched his genitals, his act was interpreted as masturbation; if he sought out his mother in bed, he was seducing her; when he embraced his playmates he was a homosexual or, if they were girls, a bigamist. To Freud, a baby's sucking, a child holding back its excreta, and adult coitus were all examples of the human striving for organ pleasure. Had he named these phenomena less provocatively, the controversies over his theories might well have been lessened—but so might their impact. Freud himself had no doubts that his generalization of sexuality was valid:

> You will perhaps protest that all this is not sexuality. I have been using the word in a far wider sense than that in which you have been accustomed to understand it. So much I am quite ready to grant you. But the question arises whether it is not rather you who have been using the word in far too narrow a sense by restricting it to the sphere of reproduction. It means that you are sacrificing an understanding of the perversions and the connection between the perversions, the neuroses and normal sexual life; and you are making it impossible for you to recognize in its true significance, the easily observable beginnings of the somatic and mental erotic life of children. But however you may choose to decide the verbal usage, you should bear firmly in mind that psycho-analysts understand sexuality in the full sense to which one is led by a consideration of infantile sexuality.[12]

Another aspect of Freud's revolutionary view of the child was that its mind was not a *tabula rasa*, nor was it filled with the innocent thoughts of an Emile; instead it was a storehouse of sexual knowledge in varying stages of completeness, which the child had put together as it strove to gain an intellectual grasp on its most urgent problems. One such problem was the arrival of a new baby, which had the effect of threatening the child's own position in the family, and which stirred it to ask where babies come from. Already it would have gleaned ideas of its own from folktales, and from observations of pregnancy and changes in family routine. The child's newly awakened curiosity demanded fresh facts, but instead of receiving a frank answer, most likely he or she would be fobbed off with the stork fable (which was likely to be rejected both instinctively and intellectually). The child experienced a psychological conflict when it adopted the "right" answers of the parents through the repression of its own more valid gropings; this could bring on states like compulsive brooding and depression, which served as substitutes for the earlier anxieties. The various incomplete ideas that children held about reproduction and birth, Freud called sexual theories, and the acute questioning accompanying them, sexual researches.

The young child's ignorance led it to speculate that the process of birth was like the evacuation of excreta, that the baby could pass out through the navel, breast, or mouth, and that the child itself could give birth in this way. Other sexual theories related to family life. If it observed sexual intercourse between the parents, the ignorant child would be likely to interpret it as an act of ill treatment and subjugation. As usual, this conclusion had some basis in observation; bloodstains could be seen on sheets, and the mother heard as she sometimes recoiled from her husband for fear of pregnancy. The child would not be surprised to learn that the quarrels of the day were carried on at night by his parents, or that they were settled in the same physical fashion in which its own disputes with playmates were resolved. These first sadistic interpretations of intercourse, with their real or imagined foundations, had power to reassert themselves in married life, where the husband might treat his wife as he imagined his father had served his mother. Where a child had no opportunity to observe parental intercourse, it could still fall victim to the interpretation, for gaps in the child's knowledge could be supplemented by the instinctual phylogenetic heritage. Freud did not doubt that things seen and dimly understood in the cradle set up elaborate networks in the mind of the child that could be reactivated and reinterpreted later.

The phylogenetic heritage, seen as an important factor shaping childhood, could also influence symbolism in language and dreams. However, Freud cautioned against resorting to it as an explanation until other possibilities had been exhausted. This late nineteenth-century idea that the racial past could help determine the present struck another blow at the innocence of childhood, for innocence could scarcely survive when, in an important sense, a child was sexually experienced in advance.

Each child's sexual theorizing was bound to end in frustration on account of the incomplete evidence available to it, the limits of its own physical development, and the dictates of reality. Freud accepted that this frustration led to the inhibition of curiosity, as well as to the loss of physical charm that characterized the onset of latency. It was also the source of complaints later that "I can't accomplish anything; I can't succeed in anything." Allowing for this, such theorizing in childhood could make a positive contribution to the child's upbringing. Little Hans's understanding of the differences between the animate and inanimate, and between the sexes, was aided by his observation of the "widdlers" of male animals, and of their absence in females and in inanimate objects.[13] Similarly, in the report Freud quoted from Ferenczi, the young neurotic Arpad, whose favorite game was slaughtering fowls, had observed the sexual life of the fowlyard with a consequent gain in biological knowledge.[14] Even anxiety situations, such as the child fearing that it would be replaced in its parents' favors by a new baby, could contribute to making the child thoughtful and clear-sighted.

Freud claimed that the vigor with which a child pursued sexual theorizing was one measure of later greatness. He made his point by suggesting that the passion for knowledge of Leonardo da Vinci could be linked to the intense sexual researches of a boyhood spent without a father. Freud also argued that these experiences were related to the content of da Vinci's art. This was also why biographers represented their heroes and heroines as cold, ideal figures; in truth, they were reviving childhood perceptions of their own long-dead fathers.

§   §   §

IN 1923, at the age of sixty-seven, Freud launched a fresh theory of human personality in *The Ego and the Id* that was of particular importance for parents and educators. In place of the simple division of mind into an ego and an unconscious, he now proposed a dynamic tripartite structure comprising the "id"—characterized by the impulses and instinctual drives of the newborn child, which lacked any directing consciousness—the "ego"—a self that had been separated and differentiated from the primeval conglomeration because of the child's need to come to terms with reality—and the "superego"—an unconscious agency in the mind with a censoring and prohibiting function. The superego was based on the internalized guilt of the Oedipus complex, and it developed further as moral concepts were built up. The original prohibitions issued by the superego were derived from the child's parents; later the superego took on the influences of those who had stepped into the place of parents: the teachers, priests, and other father substitutes. Such identifications were essential in forming the character of children.

There is an important caveat to interpose here. Freud's famous terms—id, ego, and superego—were not his, but were taken from Latin by his English translators, and have a pronounced medical ring to them. Bruno Bettelheim has argued recently that this translation completely obscures Freud's meaning:

> Only the wish to perceive psychoanalysis as a medical specialty can explain why three of Freud's most important new theoretical concepts were translated not into English but into a language whose most familiar use today may be for writing prescriptions.[15]

Bettelheim points out that the best equivalents for Freud's original German terms are "the It," "I" or "Me," and "Above-I." Thus,

> in naming two of the concepts, Freud chose words that are among the first words used by every German child. . . . To mistranslate *Ich* as "Ego" is to transform it into jargon that no longer conveys the personal commitment we make when we say "I" or "Me."[16]

Bettelheim's concerns are important; and his work is a reminder that what a model means to its creator is not always what it comes to mean for those whom it subsequently influences.

To return to the superego (retaining the now standard translation): so far as education was concerned, it acted as a restraining and conservative force. Parents and teachers generally looked to the precepts of their own superego for guidance in upbringing:

> Whatever understanding their ego may have come to with their super-ego, they are severe and exacting in educating children. They have forgotten the difficulties of their own childhood and they are glad to be able now to identify themselves fully with their own parents who in the past laid such severe restrictions upon them. Thus a child's super-ego is in fact constructed on the model not of its parents but of its parents' super-ego; the contents which fill it are the same and it becomes the vehicle of tradition and of all the time-resisting judgments of value which have propagated themselves in this manner from generation to generation.[17]

Freud soon made use of his new theory in an attempt to convince the public that anxiety in children should be regarded as a normal occurrence. Initially he had conceived it as the product of strong emotions or desires held in check; later he argued that anxiety arose, not in the unconscious mind following repression, but in the ego following the perception of danger. Every stage of childhood had its characteristic anxiety, beginning with the anxiousness of the infant in arms when it first realized it was a separate being from its mother, the shock of which gradually dissipated as it came to learn that the mother's disappearance was followed by her reappearance. The next major stage came with the child learning that the parents could be angry with it; this fear of the deprivation of love would persist throughout life in one form or another. The third period was linked with the threat of castration, and the fourth with the emergence of the superego.

> We can say that in fact a particular determinant of anxiety (that is, situation of danger) is allotted to every age of development as being appropriate to it. The danger of physical helplessness fits the stage of the ego's early immaturity; the danger of loss of an object (or loss of love) fits the lack of self-sufficiency in the first years of childhood; the danger of being castrated fits the phallic phase; and finally fear of the super-ego, which assumes a special position, fits the period of latency.[18]

As a child grew up, past anxieties, like the fear of being alone, of animals, and of strangers, usually lost their terrors. However, these early fears could sometimes combine with present stages, making it difficult, Freud declared, to reduce anxiety to a consistent typology. Parents must accept that anxiety was inherent in man's biological nature, and they would be unwise to attempt to shield their children from it by overprotection, which could heighten the fear of loss of love. Further, anxiety was indispensable in civilized society, for it was a major force in the functioning of the superego.

§   §   §

THE events that had the greatest influence on the child were the interactions within the family between child and child and between child and parent. Freud found the supposition that the fraternal relationship should be a loving one inexplicable. Both observation and the study of dreams revealed to him that the elder brother ill-treated the younger by maligning and stealing from him, while the younger was consumed with impotent rage, envy, and fear. Freud believed that the most constant source of tension in family life was the rivalry between father and son for the mother's affections, which began as soon as the father became aware of the special quality of a boy's love for his mother. The hostility arising from this, which was embedded in the unconscious, was represented in the legends of Zeus, who had emasculated his father, and Kronos, who had devoured his children. There was also hostility between mother and daughter based on the girl's longing for sexual freedom and on the woman's fear of menopause.

Freud regarded the close ties of family life—which saw fathers favor daughters, and mothers, their sons—as essentially sexual bonds. If a girl attached herself to her brother, she was seeking a father substitute; if she became close to a younger sister, she could be substituting for the vain wish of having a baby by the father. Family life was lived out in an atmosphere of love and hate. Even the very young had inexhaustibly deep emotional feelings. Freud recounted a case in which a two-year-old girl attempted to strangle an infant in its cradle because its presence had challenged her position as favorite. Such situations could take quite complicated forms. For example, if an elder child demonstrated musical ability and was admired for it, a younger might refuse to touch an instrument in retaliation, although he might be the more talented of the two.

In looking at relationships within the family, Freud accepted that a mother's love for her son was the most complete; it was the purest example of unchangeable affection, and, free from ambivalence and unimpaired by egoistical considerations, it exerted a lifelong influence on the son. Commenting on Goethe's autobiography, Freud remarked that if a man had been his mother's undisputed darling, "he retains throughout life the triumphant feeling, confidence in success, which not seldom brings actual success along with it." He thought Goethe could well have used the subtitle "My strength has its roots in my relation to my mother."[19] Freud felt that he himself had benefited from such love and that this had helped him stand against his critics. A mother transferred her ambitions to her son along with her milk. In so doing she aroused sexual excitation, teaching him how to love; and when the child learned to distinguish between nipple and self, he was beginning to discover himself as an entity. However, Freud warned against any undue protraction of this sublime mother-son accord. He argued that da Vinci's period of prolonged dependence on his mother played a part in leading the artist into homosexuality:

In all our male homosexual cases the subjects had had a very intense erotic attachment to a female person, as a rule their mother, during the first period of childhood, which is afterwards forgotten; this attachment was evoked or encouraged by too much tenderness on the part of the mother herself, and further reinforced by the small part played by the father during their childhood.[20]

The proper fate for the mother's love was repression, although its effects could usually be observed in adulthood in the male's continuing affection for his mother, which was an expression of his thwarted aim-inhibited sexual instincts.

Over the years, children must learn to live as best they could with the shortcomings of their family and its emotional crosscurrents. Harmony would increase if children learned something about what was really happening, even at the cost of more familiar relations between parent and child. For their part, parents should accept the sexual components of family life and not attempt to suppress them, for this could prevent more mature relationships from emerging at puberty.

In view of the importance of a child's relations to his parents in determining his later choice of a sexual object, it can easily be understood that any disturbance of those relations will produce the gravest effects upon his adult sexual life. Jealousy in a lover is never without an infantile root or at least an infantile reinforcement. If there are quarrels between the parents or if their marriage is unhappy, the ground will be prepared in their children for the severest predisposition to a disturbance of sexual development or to a neurotic illness.[21]

With puberty came the social duty of escaping the confines of the home. Freud welcomed the generation gap, believing that "the whole progress of society rests upon opposition between successive generations."[22] Only when a youth had learned to transfer his attachments from his mother to others did he truly enter manhood, but such independence was difficult to achieve. Those who failed to make the break would seek to model their parents in their own marriages, and this could be accompanied by an inability to relate properly to their spouses. In the fullest meaning of the expression, these people remain "in love" with their blood relations. Freud accused Viennese parents of refusing to prepare the way for their children's eventual independence, with the father taking a "head-of-the-family" posture and the mother seeking to bind her children to her by every conceivable means. The break from home was made the more difficult because in man's phylogenetic past he had been accustomed to live in primitive clusters, not in complex social organizations. Nevertheless, independence was a task set for all, and success or failure in it was an important measure of social fitness.

Overall, the best start parents could give a child would be to have themselves psychoanalyzed; this would prevent some of the neuroses that resulted from ignorance and would spare the child some of the inflictions that had been visited on them. A good home was one in which primitive "child-beasts" were turned into cultivated adults who would bring up their own children in an enlightened fashion.

§   §   §

THROUGHOUT his writing, Freud often paused to comment on points of practical concern to parents. Writing to his friend Fliess in 1897, he suggested that the symptoms of a girl with an obsessional neurosis were linked with a strict toilet-training regime. The girl, who was attending needlework classes, was obsessed by the idea "No, you mustn't go off, you haven't *finished* yet, you must make [*machen*] some more, you must learn a lot more." Freud revealed that she had been forcibly held on the potty as an infant and told, "You mustn't go off, you haven't *finished* yet, you must *do* [*machen*] some more."[23] The word *machen*, meaning both make and do, brought together the later and the infantile situations, and at a time of stress, an archaic command had emerged out of the unconscious in the form of an obsessional neurosis. Freud's analysis would have forced the girl's mother to consider whether regularity of the bowels was such a virtue if it was purchased at the expense of future mental disturbance.

The explanations Freud gave for child behavior changed over the years as his theoretical position developed. Early in his career, when he had studied bed-wetting, he was concerned with organic causation. At the time of his attachment to the seduction theory, he attributed persistent bed-wetting to sexual excitation in infancy. Later, he linked continual bed-wetting with masturbation in the young child and suggested that its suppression could invoke the threat of castration. However, Freud was consistent in that he considered its persistence a danger signal calling for therapeutic action, urging, as a general rule, that unconventional behavior in young children should never be suppressed severely and that no more coercion should be applied in the home than appeared absolutely necessary.

Freud took a conservative view of masturbation. While he accepted the habit in the young as part of the working out of infantile sexuality, he thought it an inadequate response beyond the egocentric stage—it could lead to a fixation of infantile sexual aims, which, by encouraging withdrawal from life, would make adjustment to reality more difficult. Indeed, he went on to speculate whether it was a causative agent of neurosthenia and argued that, if practiced constantly, it might lead to impotence or organic injury. It was "the first great deviation"[24] in man and "the primal addiction"[25] whose substitutes were morphine, alcohol, and tobacco. Nevertheless, Freud conceded that masturbation could be helpful in discharging the sexual emotions building up at the time of the Oedipus complex; it could alleviate the worst consequences of abstinence and, for a few, was preferable to active perversion. He also spoke of a useful return to it in the course of some therapy; and he speculated that the diminution of male potency accompanying it could be useful to civilization by reducing aggression.

Freud's readers were urged not to suppress too severely those children who masturbated, for this could encourage sadism, as in the Wolf-man case. Its suppression here had preceded a sadistic and anal period in which the child tormented his nurse, delighted in cruelties like pulling wings off flies, and engaged in fantasies of beating. The guilt connected with masturbation was especially strong, Freud maintained, because it was associated with the guilt of the Oedipus situation. Granted his reservations, Freud had little sympathy for those who attributed everything to the habit, from falling hair to bankruptcy; and when discussing its effects, he was careful to argue within the context of his broader sexual theories, asserting that the precise nature of masturbation's harmfulness would have to wait on the solution of the problem of when sexual activity became pathogenic.

§   §   §

FREUD claimed that the severe effects of some of the neuroses afflicting his patients could have been avoided by adequate sex education. Nineteenth-century parents generally considered sex a topic taboo for family discussion, believing that information about it could arouse the instinct prematurely (an attitude that apparently persists today). The parents' implicit assumption was that if they withheld knowledge, it would not reach their children, and that they would in fact be retarding its acquisition. Parents did not consider that their children would have a natural interest in the topic. According to Freud, the truth lay in the opposite direction. The newborn baby brings sexuality with it into the world, he affirmed, and children experience strong sexually based feelings of love, tenderness, devotion, and jealousy long before puberty. Instead of providing any guarantee of purity, sexual ignorance stimulated unhealthy curiosity, which a child would satisfy in secret. At the same time, the child would learn that everything sexual was disgusting.

To support his point that children often felt a tormenting curiosity about sex, Freud published the letter of a motherless eleven-year-old girl who had been speculating on the question of the origin of babies:[26]

> DEAR AUNT MALI,
>   Will you please be so kind as to tell me how you got Cristel and Paul. You must know because you are married. We were arguing about it yesterday evening and we want to know the truth. We have nobody else to ask. When are you coming to Salzberg? You know, Aunt Mali, we simply can't understand how the stork brings babies. Trudel thought the stork brings them in a shirt. Then we want to know as well if the stork gets them out of the pond and why one never sees babies in ponds. And will you please tell me too, how one knows beforehand when one is going to have one. Write and tell me everything about it.
>   With thousands of greetings and kisses from us all.
>
>   Your inquisitive niece,
>   LILI

The answer Lili and Trudel received was apparently inadequate because later in life Lili developed an obsessional brooding that Freud attributed to such unconscious unanswered questions. A. S. Neill had a similar view, and quoted parallel cases from his experiences at Summerhill, such as the small boy who deluged him with questions: "What did you pay for that clock?" "What time is it?" "When does the school term end?" The boy was full of anxiety, Neill noted, and was "evading the big question that he wanted to have answered."

> One day, he came to my room and asked a string of questions. I made no reply, and went on reading my book. After a dozen questions, I looked up casually and said, "What was that you asked? Where do babies come from?"

The boy stormed out of the room, only to return after a few minutes to hear Neill's answer.[27]

The significance that Freud placed on sex education came out in the Little Hans analysis, which was undertaken by the boy's father under Freud's guidance. In his attempt to give the boy some conscious grasp of his unconscious wishes, the father had explained some facts of life as the treatment proceeded. Freud claimed he himself would have gone further by introducing the anxious five-year-old to the existence of the vagina and of copulation. At this time Freud accepted that the specific facts of human sexuality ought to be given by the age of ten at school and that children should learn the moral obligations of sex at the time of confirmation. Over the years, though, Freud became less certain of the efficacy of early sex education. Some thirty years after the Little Hans analysis he wrote:

> I am far from maintaining that this is a harmful or unnecessary thing to do, but it is clear that the prophylactic effect of this literal measure has been greatly over-estimated. After such enlightenment, children know something they did not know before, but they make no use of that new knowledge that has been presented to them. We come to see that they are not even in so great a hurry to sacrifice for this new knowledge the sexual theories which might be described as a natural growth and which they have constructed in harmony with, and dependence on, their imperfect libidinal organization—theories about the part played by the stork, about the nature of sexual intercourse and about the way in which babies are made.[28]

§   §   §

A FURTHER important insight that set Freudian theory apart from alternative theories of upbringing was his contention that when a child misbehaved it could be for a reason the child itself did not comprehend. While such misbehavior had its source in the unconscious, it was not irrational in the sense of not having a cause, for Freud considered that human acts were never arbitrary. Analysis could reveal that a child who had stolen money from her father was acting from motives of genuine love, or that a child who lied and boasted of her father at school was really motivated by a desire to belittle him. Similarly, Goethe's childhood act of smashing dishes and cooking pots by throwing them out of an upstairs window was actually an expression of his jealousy as an elder brother seeking to get rid of a younger one. Analytic theory suggested that delinquency could be traced to the sense of guilt coming from the killing of the father in the racial past, as well as other reasons. Acts of theft, fraud, and arson could well bring relief to the child by enabling him to attach his Oedipal guilt to real life situations—in other words, children could be naughty just to provoke punishment. The same desire for punishment sometimes motivated adults to admit to crimes of which they were not guilty. Freud warned the judiciary that the confessions of criminals, like the weeping of children, should not be taken as proof of complicity in particular misdeeds. His arguments had the effect of minimizing the child's responsibility for its own actions and thus further undermined the traditional and orthodox view of child culpability. In similar vein, A. S. Neill sometimes rewarded children who were thieves or were antisocial.

On the whole, though, Freud had little tolerance for permissive upbringing. If parents spoiled children they would exacerbate fears of the loss of love, and this would encourage individuals to remain in a childlike state characterized by motor and psychical helplessness. The child would be fearful away from adults and would turn into a parent who would spoil his or her own children. The effects of spoiling were a contagion, diverting individuals from the task of learning to live in a universe that offered no consolation. Yet at the same time Freud rejected corporal punishment, especially if severely or unjustly administered, claiming that he knew of a case where unjust punishment helped turn a wild but self-confident child into a shy, timid person who was unable to manage her own affairs. He also thought—learning from Rousseau—that spanking on the buttocks could encourage masochism.

§   §   §

AN important assumption underlying a great deal of Freud's theorizing was that he was describing males. In 1900 he considered that the psychology of women could be taken as analogous to that of men, but he was to abandon this position later and maintain that, strictly speaking, the Oedipus complex applied only to boys. In summary, Freud argued that the crisis in a girl's life came when she realized that she had no penis. The shock of this, coming before the Oedipus situation, was accompanied by a belief that she was castrated. Her immediate reaction was to turn from her mother to her father. In changing her love object, the girl gave up old habits of clitoral stimulation and wished for a baby from the father. The shift marked a renunciation of the active masculine trait of masturbation in favor of the passive feminine urge that valued the vagina for its reproductive function. Because love of the father was incestuous, it had to be relinquished; however, it could not be terminated by the fear of castration, as with a boy, for the castration situation had *already* occurred. Instead, the girl's incestuous feelings were given up gradually, repressed during the period of latency. This suppression was less decisive than the fear of castration, hence the girl's longing for her father was abandoned more painfully and slowly. If the repressions of latency proved inadequate, Freud argued that a girl would either identify with her father and take on a masculine personality or regress to her first infatuation with her mother and turn homosexual, or she could repudiate sexuality altogether. By this stage in his career Freud had accepted that "Anatomy is Destiny."[29]

Rousseau had treated women as Emile's social inferiors, and Wesley, while rejecting much of Rousseau's thought, would have agreed with him. But probably both would have been amazed by Freud's psychological and organic theory that a major source of feminine inferiority was the lack of a penis. According to Freud, this deficiency was soon discovered by boys, who believed that their female playmates had been castrated and held them in lower regard because of it. This vital deficiency was the true cause of female inferiority and of a woman's subservient position in society; it also played a part in her jealousy, and in female vanity, which was a form of overcompensation. Furthermore, because a female could not terminate her Oedipal stage as decisively as the male, her capacity for sexual sublimation was lessened, and consequently her ethical and moral structures were less substantial. Freud explained:

> The castration complex prepares for the Oedipus complex instead of destroying it; the girl is driven out of her attachment to her mother through the influence of her envy for the penis and she enters the Oedipus situation as though into a haven of refuge. In the absence of fear of castration the chief motive is lacking which leads boys to surmount the Oedipus complex. Girls remain in it for an indeterminate length of time; they demolish it late and, even so, incompletely. In these circumstances the formation of the super-ego must suffer; it cannot attain the strength and independence which give it its cultural significance, and feminists are not pleased when we point out to them the effects of this factor upon the average feminine character.[30]

Thus the influence of womanhood was a force against civilization. Women also sought to keep men at home and in thrall by the promise of satiating their sexual needs. The reason that women's success was less than complete was because they were emotionally unstable and dependent on the male. To Freud, equality of the sexes was an absurd notion.

However, not all differences between the sexes worked against girls. A little girl's greater need for affection and approval made her more outgoing and intelligent than a boy of the same age, and this active seeking of love led her to control her bowels more easily and quickly. Girls also showed a commendable spirit of independence when they rebelled against their mothers, and because their sexual expression took a passive form, their natures were less sadistic. Unfortunately, their early intellectual flowering seldom survived the repressions of latency. A woman's fate was to regress toward identification with her mother. By the age of thirty her thinking was rigidified, her closed mind evident in her willingness to accept a monarchy and religion.

For all this, Freud was never sure of the validity of his theories where women were concerned. They were the "dark continent" of psychology, and he advised men who wished to understand them better to either await the advance of science or to look to the poets or to their own experiences!

Freud also believed that any discussion of the differences between the sexes had to take account of human bisexuality. He rejected simplistic arguments that boys were masculine and girls feminine, asserting that all children had elements of both in their makeup and that neither quality was found unalloyed in either a biological or psychological sense. This notion of bisexuality was integral to his Oedipus theory with its alternative feminine and masculine dispositions. The message for parents was to avoid treating their children according to conventional preconceptions and thus sexually polarizing them at an early age; they must expect boys to show feminine attitudes at times, and girls, masculine ones. He thought it better for the child to be considered in terms of such bisexuality until the unique balance was realized at puberty.

§   §   §

IN discussing psychoanalysis and upbringing, Freud could scarcely avoid commenting on the relationship of his science to formal education. While he averred that he had contributed "nothing to the application of analysis to education," he had suggested earlier in his career that psychoanalytic treatment was akin to a second education that would serve as a corrective to schooling. This led to some misunderstandings, and he made the point later that the education of children was something quite separate from psychoanalysis, which could aid—but not replace—education. When presenting this modest claim, Freud championed the findings of his daughter Anna Freud, who had made the study of the relationship of psychoanalysis and education her life's work, and also the achievements of Mrs. Melanie Klein, Pastor Oskar Pfister, and Dr. Hug-Hellmuth. Freud always had encouragement for those who chose to work in the first of the "three impossible professions—educating, healing and governing."[31]

Freud suggested a number of general ways in which psychoanalysis could be used to serve the ends of education. It was important in redirecting children who had deviated from the normal course of development but who were not seriously neurotic, as A. S. Neill found. It also served a prophylactic function, ideally reducing instances of accidental trauma in childhood, remembering, of course, that it could not touch the inaccessible constituents of man's insubordinate instincts. Freud realized that the spread of psychoanalysis in education depended on committed teachers, and he argued that laymen who were familiar with it should have the right to practice in schools.

In appraising the early education of Little Hans, Freud echoed Rousseau with his point that Hans was a "cheerful, straightforward child, and so he should have been, considering the education given him by his parents, which consisted essentially in the omission of our usual educational sins."[32] Like Rousseau, he argued that education in the past had done great damage. He claimed that experience had taught educators that the sexual will of the new generation would only prove tractable if influenced very early. Hence sexual activities were frowned on, and education attempted to retard sexual development by suppressing the instincts. However, no account was taken of the psychological cost of that suppression.

Freud also took issue with the "premature religious influence"[33] in education and predicted that reform in education was unlikely if it remained in the hands of the clergy. Freud was openly skeptical of religion's claim of promoting morality. In worshipping God, man was merely invoking a substitute for the overenhanced father of childhood. Those unenlightened by psychoanalysis still clung to their gods as compensation for the renunciation of the instinctual pleasures and to exorcize the terrors of nature and reconcile themselves to death. Religion relied for much of its persuasiveness on the sense of guilt arising from the Oedipus situation, which was the historical source of original sin. Freud did grant a limited usefulness to religion insofar as it helped to suppress instinctual impulses, although the frequency of religious backsliding suggested that it was less than wholly successful.

Lastly, Freud declared that contemporary educators were failing to prepare the young for the existence of aggression in life. Children were taught that other people followed ethical codes and were virtuous. In this way educators set up a false psychological orientation in children that was equivalent to equipping a polar expedition with summer clothing and maps of the Italian lakes. It would be better to say "This is how men ought to be, in order to be happy and to make others happy; but you have to reckon on their not being like that."[34] While Freud accepted that some progress in education required reconstruction of the foundations of the social system, he did not think psychoanalysis should be directed against existing society. Its aim should be restricted to making children healthy and efficient, for in itself psychoanalysis contained "enough revolutionary factors to ensure that no one educated by it will in later life take the side of reaction and suppression. It is even my opinion that revolutionary children are not desirable from any point of view."[35]

In Freud's estimation, his method was directed to turning the child into a civilized, useful member of society with the least possible sacrifice of its own activity. Unless the child learned to control its instincts, life would prove impossible for its parents and itself. Accepting that the major task of education was to "inhibit, forbid and suppress,"[36] Freud recognized that the suppression of the instincts did involve the risk of neurotic illness. Hence educators must skirt "the Scylla of non-interference and the Charybdis of frustration"[37] in their search for an education that would achieve the most with the least damage. They must take into account also that children have "very different innate constitutional dispositions so that it is quite impossible that the same educational procedure can be equally good for all children."[38] Each child needed a unique balance of love and authority, a mix that could be attained only by psychoanalytic insights into the working of the immature mind.

Nonetheless, an ideal upbringing was unattainable, for mankind's capacity for education was circumscribed by its own nature. While education could help build up mental forces like shame, disgust, and morality, which could impede the sexual instinct, the basis of repression during a child's growth was organically determined and fixed by heredity, and it would occur without assistance from education at all. More broadly, education served social ends by working to restrain sexual activity until a degree of intellectual maturity had been reached. Thus it played its part in diverting people from sexual activities, thereby keeping the population down, as well as directing energy to the work of maintaining civilization.

The Freudian explanation of the school scene could scarcely have been further from the activity in which the Arnoldean headmaster thought himself engaged. The headmaster and his teachers were loved, hated, and criticized, not on their own account or for their actions, but because they were father substitutes. Sport was not so much character building as an autoerotic activity. The virtues of thrift and orderliness were expressions of infantile anal eroticism; while ambition owed its origins, not to service to God, King, and Country, or even Mammon, but to a strong urethral-erotic disposition. In setting up virtuous models of conduct, teachers misled pupils, for the foundation of goodness was the reaction formation of sexual excitation.

Intellectual commitment had similar foundations: the cut and thrust of academic debate could be an expression of sexual rivalry, and sexual eruptions were linked with the tension of examinations. Once again Freud quoted Rousseau, who had been obliged to listen to the taunts of a lady he had failed to satisfy: "Give up women and study mathematics."[39] Freud also cited the case of a man who took flight from sexual desire by throwing himself into mathematical and geometric calculations, until one day his powers of apprehension were paralyzed in the face of some seemingly innocent problems: "Two bodies come together, one with a speed of . . . etc.," and "On a cylinder, the diameter of whose surface is m, describe a cone . . . etc."[40] The young man felt himself betrayed by these sexual allusions, and took flight from this subject too.

Beating, far from improving children, could arouse sexual excitation along with fear, and its long-term effects could prove much more damaging because the buttocks were a zone associated with the instinct of cruelty. Cooperation and a sense of justice in children grew out of the murderous rivalries of early childhood, which had to be abandoned and replaced by identification with older children. Envy and jealousy were the bases of later virtue. The rages of pupils and students were depicted by Freud as healthy outbursts of revolt against the compulsions of logic and reality—they represented attempts by students to rescue a little of the freedom of thought they were being deprived of by academic discipline. Finally, Freud rejected the idea that the school should implant the social ideas of the parents; rather, it should seek to support its pupils at a time when their development required them to relax the ties of home and family.

§   §   §

FREUD'S discoveries about childhood, he maintained, came principally from self-analysis, from analyses of adults, and from material collected from his own family and friends. Comparatively little was derived directly from the analysis of children, although Freud especially prized material from this source and used it to support his theoretical constructs as well as to attack the theories of rival analysts. He claimed that such material had the advantage of allowing firsthand observation of the working of relatively uncomplicated sexual impulses, although he recognized special difficulties in regard to both its paucity and its possible adult-suggested source. Freud accepted that an understanding of child psychology would serve the same function that research in the development of lower animals had performed for research in the higher; indeed, he considered that in his own lifetime children had replaced adults as the most suitable and important subjects for psychoanalytic research.

Freud insisted that questions of scientific methodology, and about the validity of his theory, were subordinate in his thinking—it was the therapeutic goals and successful cures that justified his work. Many philosophers and psychologists who came later were not as convinced; the fact that psychoanalytic methods sometimes work is no evidence that the theory is true. Freud's theories certainly "explain" the case material that he cites by way of example, but only in a loose sense of the term. His theories do not permit the making of precise predictions—an integral aspect of science; and for the same reason, his theories are not testable. In order to be testable a theory must be incompatible with some possible and observable events; a tester must be able to see if the predicted rather than the incompatible event occurs in some artfully contrived experiment or naturalistic setting. For this reason some recent writers regard Freud's work as pre-science; others regard it as akin to poetry or religion. Bettelheim, for example, argues "how deeply humane a person Freud was."

> He was a humanist in the best sense of the word. His greatest concern was with man's innermost being, to which he most frequently referred through the use of a metaphor—man's soul—because the word "soul" evokes so many emotional connotations. . . . Instead of instilling a deep feeling for what is most human in all of us, the translations attempt to lure the reader into developing a "scientific" attitude toward man and his actions.[41]

Freud certainly hoped that parents and laymen would take up his ideas, and he promised that those who did would find ways of guiding their children with a minimum of psychological damage from the stone-age barbarism of infancy to the maturity of participation in civilization. Unhappily, a small minority of children would remain asocial; nevertheless, if psychoanalytic insights were applied extensively, mankind could expect to move closer to a utopian age in which kindness, hard work, and reason would rule.

6.

THE AGES OF MAN: FROM GENESIS TO PIAGET

AT the time Freud was writing, psychologists, educationists, and child-care experts were showing increasing interest in the stages of growth of the normal child. Although children had come under the close scrutiny of their elders through the ages, no general agreement had yet been reached on such an apparently simple matter as the number of stages that were passed through. One could almost pick a favorite number and find a theory to support it. For example, primitive cultures usually recognized two main stages of development, childhood and maturity, the border between them often being demarcated by ritual ceremonies. In medieval times, in some circles, there were held to be seven ages of man, which paralleled the Biblical days of Creation and which also was in harmony with the number of prominent celestial bodies. This view was reflected by Shakespeare in *As You Like It*:

> At first the infant,
> Mewling and puking in the nurse's arms.
> And then the whining schoolboy, with his satchel
> And shining morning face, creeping like a snail
> Unwillingly to school. And then the lover,
> Sighing like a furnace, with a woeful ballad
> Made to his mistress' eyebrow. Then a soldier,
> Full of strange oaths, and bearded like the pard,
> Jealous in honor, sudden and quick in quarrel,
> Seeking the bubble reputation
> Even in the cannon's mouth. And then the justice,
> In fair round belly with good capon lin'd,
> With eyes severe and beard of formal cut,

Full of wise saws and modern instances;
And so he plays his part. The sixth age shifts
Into the lean and slipper'd pantaloon,
With spectacles on nose, and pouch on side,
His youthful hose, well sav'd, a world too wide
For his shrunk shank, and his big manly voice,
Turning again toward childish treble, pipes
And whistles in his sound. Last scene of all,
That ends this strange eventful history,
Is second childishness, and mere oblivion,
Sans teeth, sans eyes, sans taste, sans everything.[1]

Rousseau, in the eighteenth century, described Emile as passing through four main stages; and in the nineteenth century, the philosopher Auguste Comte asserted that mankind had passed through three historical stages, an argument that was used to show that there were three main stages of intellectual growth in the individual.

Not until the late eighteenth century did empirical research into the growth of children have its humble start.[2] By the late nineteenth century it was gaining impetus, and a survey of major research journals revealed thirty-five empirical studies in the period 1890 to 1899; but from 1950 to 1958 the number was 362, while a peak of 491 was reached in the years 1930 through 1939.[3]

§   §   §

HISTORIANS of child psychology usually credit Dietrich Tiedemann with being the pioneer in the field of scientific description of development during early childhood. Tiedemann observed his son for a short period, and in a report published in 1787 anticipated that his preliminary observations would be rectified in time by keener and more conscientious observers.[4] But Tiedemann's words were misleading—his essay did not simply report his objective observations. He did not appreciate the methodological point that theory and observation are interrelated; in any situation there are innumerable things to observe, but most are ignored because the investigator has accepted a paradigm or model that acts as a framework directing attention to particular problems. Furthermore, the investigator's theoretical framework may well determine the terminology that is adopted to describe the observations. The aspects of child development that engaged Tiedemann's attention, and the language in which he couched his work, indicate that he certainly worked from a clear-cut theoretical framework.

Tiedemann was a follower of Locke. It is speculative to suggest that his motive in studying his son was to illustrate Locke's contention that "he that attentively considers the state of a child, at his first coming into the world, will have little reason to think him stored with plenty of ideas, that are to be the matter of his future knowledge. It is by *degrees* he comes to be furnished with them."[5] Nevertheless, such a theoretical position certainly influenced Tiedemann's observations. He believed, for example, that he had observed "the association of ideas" when the infant stopped crying because it had been placed upon its side in the position of nursing; he did not realize that the actual observation was merely the cessation of crying in a particular position, and the rest, a theoretical interpretation. Similarly, Tiedemann was blind to the influence of theoretical presuppositions when he wrote that the fact that babies turn their eyes to the light was "a proof that light makes upon them a pleasing impression."[6] Perhaps the Lockean flavor of Tiedemann's work is most readily apparent in the following passage:

> The first bodily movements are merely mechanical, according to physical stimulations; from this the mind obtains ideas of motions to be performed with the limbs; then desires awaken, which by the help of association produce intentional actions; experience imparts a knowledge of the various sorts of motion, and teaches us to project our energies into the requisite parts of the body.[7]

Almost a century later, a rival to the Lockean child described by Tiedemann appeared in Wilhelm Preyer's account of the development of his son, published in 1881 as *The Mind of the Child*. Preyer admitted that many workers had made "occasional observations in regard to many children," but he stressed the paucity of detailed chronological studies of individual children.[8] He kept a diary of observations during his son's first three years, using a crude version of the modern time-sampling technique by observing his son at three regular times during the day. Preyer also set out his work under useful headings: first, he dealt with the development of the senses, taking each in turn; then he treated development of the will, including here reflex and conscious activity; finally, he dealt with development of the intellect.

The methodological features of Preyer's book reflected his scientific training—he was Professor of Physiology at Jena. However, with respect to the distinction between observation and theory, his work was almost as lacking in sophistication as Tiedemann's in the previous century. Even the preface to his book illustrates that theoretical beliefs influenced his observations; the essential difference between Tiedemann and himself was his rejection of the former's Lockean framework:

> The mind of the new-born child, then, does not resemble a *tabula rasa*, upon which the senses first write their impressions, so that out of these the sum-total of our mental life arises through manifold reciprocal action, but the tablet is already written upon before birth, with many illegible, nay unrecognizable and invisible marks, the traces of the print of countless sensuous impressions of long-gone generations. So blurred and indistinct are these remains, that we might, indeed, suppose the tablet to be blank, so long as we did not examine the changes it undergoes in earliest youth.[9]

In Preyer's time, the University of Jena was one of the sites of Continental opposition to Lockean empiricism, for the University had links with Leibniz, who had studied there, and Herbart, some of whose disciples taught there. Both of these men had denied that the developing child was a passive receptor of sense impressions, and they emphasized the activity of the developing mind—the ability of the perceiver to control, select, and organize.

Preyer's theoretical model did not dispose him to regard the mind of the child as an entity worthy of study for its own sake. He ignored Rousseau's message that "childhood has its own ways of seeing, thinking, and feeling,"[10] and he approached the child from the point of view of an adult, asking when and in what order the child would display various adult abilities. Almost another half-century was to pass before Piaget came to study the abilities of children as distinctive in their own right, and until that time, Preyer's view of the child as having inborn capacities that were developed in definite stages gained many supporters.

§   §   §

AN even greater influence, however, was exerted by Preyer's contemporary, Charles Darwin. As Preyer himself put it,

> If a new sun had appeared in the sky, the astonishment of educated men from San Francisco to Moscow, from Melbourne to Bergen could hardly have been greater than it was then. The

effect of *The Origin of Species* can be compared with that of a great
fire that burns up the old parchments of natural history.[11]

The revolutionary impact of the *Origin* was felt as much in psychology
and the infant field of child study as in the biological sciences, geology,
and theology; and Darwin's later work, *The Descent of Man* (1871),
together with *The Expression of the Emotions in Man and Animals* (1872),
also played its part.[12] At a time when mankind had been viewed as
being in some sense outside nature, it had not been realistic to attempt
to understand human psychology by studying that of animals, but
with the theory of evolution a new avenue of investigation opened
up. Now it was not only the adult form of a species that was to be
studied for clues to evolutionary history—the immature forms, particularly the adaptive value of their main features and the change
undergone during their development to maturity, could be expected
to reveal much of importance.

Darwin also contributed directly to child study. He had made a
series of observations on his own children which he eventually used
in *Expression of Emotions*, and in 1877 he worked through his old notes
once more and prepared a short paper entitled "A Biographical Sketch
of an Infant" after reading an article on a similar topic by Taine in
the journal *Mind*. In his opening paragraph, Darwin revealed that
one main point of interest for him was the manner of acquisition of
typical adult faculties. He wrote, "I feel sure, from what I have seen
with my own infants, that the period of development of the several
faculties will be found to differ considerably in different infants."[13]
The organization of his material reflected this interest. Darwin opened
by discussing the reflex actions and the vision of the infant, and then
he wrote in turn on "anger," "fear," "pleasurable sensations," "affection," "association of ideas, reason, etc.," "moral sense," "uncon-
sciousness, shyness," and concluded with "means of communication."
Under each of these headings he described the observable reactions
of his son from birth until past the age of two years and occasionally
made comparisons with the behavior of animals. As one commentator
has remarked, the study clearly shows the evolutionist at work.[14]

The studies made by Tiedemann, Preyer, and Darwin had at
least one methodological feature in common. All three accounts of
children centered around the development of adult faculties, for the
observers approached child study with the advantage of hindsight
and assumed the child would eventually develop into an adult pos-
sessing particular faculties. It was only on the precise nature of these
faculties that the three disagreed. From certain points of view, the

approach that Tiedemann, Preyer, and Darwin shared was an important one that resulted in useful—if somewhat differing—classifications
and accounts of the stages of child development. But it was only one
of many possible approaches. Other workers, with varying theoretical
backgrounds or points of interest, were to produce completely different classifications.

§   §   §

THE major figure among the many involved in the study of child
development in the twentieth century has been Swiss psychologist
and "genetic epistemologist" Jean Piaget. He regarded himself, in
some ways, as the intellectual successor to his illustrious countryman,
and it was fitting that for many years he was head of the Jean Jacques
Rousseau Institute in Geneva. The common thread linking the work
of the two men across the centuries was their willingness to accept
children as functioning beings in their own right—they should not
be thought of merely as immature adults, having imperfect adult
capacities. Like other living creatures, children have to survive in the
world around them; and their ways of thinking, although different
from those of adults, allow them to get by and so are of great intrinsic
interest. Whether consciously or not (at least at first), Piaget can be
conceived as devoting his adult life to amplifying Rousseau's dictum:

> I am far from thinking, however, that children have no sort of
> reason. On the contrary, I think they reason very well with regard
> to things that affect their actual and sensible well-being. But peo-
> ple are mistaken as to the extent of their information, and they
> attribute to them knowledge they do not possess, and make them
> reason about things they cannot understand.[15]

Piaget's early training was as a biologist—he was an expert on
the evolution of mollusks—and this disposed him to think in terms
of the biological structures that enable an organism to deal effectively
with its environment. Shortly after completing his doctorate, a for-
tuitous circumstance enabled him to apply his theoretical framework
to children's thought patterns: he was hired to do research to improve
the Simon and Binet intelligence test. Piaget's job was to interview
children to determine the effectiveness of the "distractors," the wrong
alternative answers on the intelligence test. (A test of this sort is
effective only if a certain proportion of the alternatives offered in each
question are challenging; if all test-takers choose the right answer, or

if all select an incorrect one, that particular question will usually need some revision.) As a result of these interviews with children, Piaget became interested in the thought patterns used to arrive at the wrong answers, which he often found to be intriguing. Piaget did *not* regard the childish errors as merely silly; rather he thought he detected a distinct nonadult "logic" at work.

Thus started the evolution of Piaget's work with children. Making good use of his own offspring, he perfected the "clinical interview," in which he would set a child a simple problem and then discuss it in such a way as to reveal (apparently) the child's thought patterns. If the child was very young, he would manipulate the situation so as to reveal as much as possible, nonverbally. The following episode is typical. Piaget was questioning a girl who was nearly seven to see if she was able to think relativistically. Piaget started by asking her what a "sister" is:

> *A sister is a girl.* —Are all girls sisters? —*Yes.* —Am I a sister? —*No.* —How do you know that I am not a sister? —*I don't know.* —But I have got a sister, then aren't I her sister? —*Oh, yes.* — What is a sister? —*A girl.* —What must you have to be a sister? —*I don't know.* (Ba [the girl here] has two sisters and a brother).[16]

A mass of data along these lines led Piaget to conclude that the cognitive repertoire of children does not include the basic "logical capacities" found in adults—children are not able to take other points of view, they are not able to reverse mental operations, they do not have facility with the logic of class inclusion, they do not, at first, know that mass and volume are conserved during alterations of physical shape (as when a ball of clay is rolled out into a sausage). Indeed, much as Locke had depicted, the child at birth had no ideas but was merely a bundle of reflexes. Everything had to be learned by interaction with, or exploration of, the environment. Even such basic notions as object-permanence—the notion that physical objects persist over time and still exist when they are out of sight—had to be learned by the infant. Piaget's typical exploration of this sort of issue with very young children went as follows:

> *Observation 59*: Lucienne at 1;1 [one year; one month] finds a watch chain in my fist. I then replace the chain in my hand and slip this hand under a pillow. I leave the chain under the pillow and bring my hand out closed. *First attempt*: Lucienne looks in my hand, then finding nothing, looks at me, laughing. She resumes searching, then gives up. *Attempts 2–5*: Same reactions. I use the watch

instead of the chain to increase her interest; same difficulty. *Sixth attempt*: This time, sudden success.[17]

Piaget eventually conceptualized development as a process in which each child constructed for itself a set of mental or cognitive structures, with the aid of which it could interact fruitfully with its surroundings—the environment could be "assimilated" by the child. Whenever a difficulty was encountered, it threw the child out of mental equilibrium, and the child was then forced to make some addition to its mental apparatus; cognitive accommodation occurred, and the child moved on to a new equilibrium. It was a thoroughly biological model, and as should be apparent, Piaget's terminology— "structure," "assimilation," "accommodation," "equilibration"—was taken over from that discipline. Piaget was quite explicit about his opinion that psychological mechanisms were only a variety of biological ones:

> In order to compare cognitive and biologic mechanisms, we must first state that the former are an extension and utilization of organic autoregulations, of which they are a form of endproduct. . . . Or in other words, that at the same time that the *cognitive structures* are an elaboration of organic structures in general, they fulfill particular functions.[18]

The most famous aspect of Piaget's theory was also heavily biological in conception—he divided development into a number of stages and even suggested rough age-ranges for each. He was clear that child growth was a continuous process; the stages were not as discrete as, for example, the stages in the life cycle of an insect. First came the "sensorimotor period," in which the behavior of the child was an outcome of inherited reflexes and patterns of action. Piaget discriminated six substages here, which infants typically took about two years to pass through. The next major period, which had two important subperiods, lasted from about two until eleven; during these years the child acquired "operational groupings" of ideas concerning objects that can be manipulated, or known through the senses. The child was able to solve simple problems, but only ones dealing with concrete issues—abstract problem solving was still not possible. Hence the name given to this general phase: the period of "concrete operations." Finally came the "formal operations" period, lasting from about the age of eleven until the age of fifteen. During this period formal thought was perfected and the development of reflective thought was completed.[19] In recent decades, neo-Piagetian researchers have paid more attention to late adolescent and even adult intellectual development.

It is important not to misinterpret the status of this stage theory. As one commentator has put it, Piaget

> does not consider the delineation of developmental stages to be an end in itself. On the contrary, the classification of stages is a means to the end of understanding the developmental process in rather the same way that zoological and botanical classification is a first step in the analysis and understanding of biological phenomena.[20]

Thanks to the stream of work coming out of Geneva for half a century or so, a great deal has been discovered about child development. But it is not surprising that gaps and deficiencies are now being revealed in the Piagetian model. After all, as the philosopher of science Sir Karl Popper has pointed out, all of our theories are fated to be overthrown, because, most likely, none of them is true! Of course, over long ages our theories may approach closer to the truth; in Popper's terminology, they increase in verisimilitude.

One limitation in Piaget's work was that he was focusing upon cognitive development; a researcher cannot hope to do everything, and Piaget chose to concentrate upon this because he felt it was central—how the child behaves in most situations is presumably influenced by how the child has *thought about* those situations. But there are other facets to consider, and the contrast with the work of Erik Erikson is revealing. Here, the theoretical framework was psychoanalytic theory, and it is not surprising that the developmental stages he outlined differed markedly from Piaget's. Whereas Piaget saw maturity in terms of the attainment of equilibrium of intellectual structures, Erikson saw it as involving the attainment of "ego integrity," which necessitated the individual's passing through seven preliminary stages. At each stage, the individual was faced by certain types of conflict that had to be resolved; for example, the first stage involved the conflict "trust versus basic mistrust," and the second, "autonomy versus shame and doubt." If the conflict in a particular stage was satisfactorily resolved, a new quality was added to the ego. The result was seen in the eighth and final stage:

> Each individual, to become a mature adult, must to a sufficient degree develop all the ego qualities mentioned, so that a wise Indian, a true gentleman, and a mature peasant share and recognize in one another the final stage of integrity. But each cultural

entity, to develop the particular style of integrity suggested by its historical place, utilizes a particular combination of these conflicts, along with specific provocations and prohibitions of infantile sexuality.[21]

Whatever conclusions are reached about Erikson's theory, it serves as a salutary reminder that individuals are multifaceted, and there is more that might have developed, apart from cognition.

Other defects in Piaget's work remain to be mentioned.[22] First, Piaget tended to regard the child as a solitary inquirer, as a "young scientist" engaged in single-handedly building his or her own cognitive structures so as to come into equilibrium with the environment. Other workers—for example, the Soviet psychologists Luria and Vygotsky—have emphasized more the role of social forces in shaping the child's cognitive growth. For most children do not develop alone; parents, teachers, older siblings, and peers indicate to the child what mental accommodations are likely to be fruitful, and they discourage the acceptance of other conceptualizations. Piaget certainly mentioned these things, but he never paid a great deal of attention to them.

Further, Piaget did not make enough of an effort to validate his theories by looking for alternative or rival explanations and then devising careful experiments to test whether his views were more adequate. In the last fifteen years or so, a number of experimentalists have taken this important step, and Piaget's ideas have not always withstood serious testing.[23]

Finally, Piaget's theory, considered solely on its merits as a theory, has been subjected to serious theoretical criticism. The mechanisms that he postulated to explain cognitive development—assimilation, accommodation, and the rest—do not appear to be adequate. Indeed, it is not clear they *explain* anything at all: to say that development occurs because the child accommodates is merely to say that the child changes because he or she changes, and to talk in terms of restoring mental equilibrium is an enticing, but in the end unsatisfactory, metaphor.

Despite all this, however, the model was a major contribution, and like all important models it enabled many investigators to notice phenomena that would otherwise have remained hidden, and it posed problems that led science into new domains.

§   §   §

How can a choice be made between the work of Tiedemann, Preyer,

Darwin, Piaget, Erikson, and others? Which account of child development is the most adequate? At the outset it is not apparent that a choice *must* be made. If several investigators produce different answers to one problem, and if the problem is known to have only one answer, then it can be confidently asserted that, at the most, only one of the rival accounts is correct. But is there only one answer to the problem of the nature of child development? Again, were different investigators necessarily rivals at all—might not they have been attempting different things? It is extremely difficult to evaluate this possibility, although in the cases of Piaget and Erikson it does appear at first sight to be well-grounded, with Erikson looking at ego development and Piaget attempting the quite different task of delineating the development of intellectual mechanisms. But even here, as in the cases of Tiedemann, Preyer, and Darwin, it is difficult to be certain.

The terms used by these workers in giving their accounts of children reflect serious differences in their theoretical views, and it is possible that, rather than attempting different things in the way that chemists and physicists attempt to answer different questions about the same substance, they were attempting the same thing but approaching the task from different theoretical positions, as happens when physicists put forward rival theories. In the physical sciences such theoretical differences are open to the possibility of resolution, for the disputants at least accept the same conceptual framework or paradigm that acts, in effect, as a basic set of rules determining what solutions are adequate and what types of argument can be put forward. But this is not the case in the social or human sciences, where there are still many arguments about the nature of the basic conceptual framework or rules. Thus, it is possible for the intellectual descendants of Locke and Darwin to denigrate the work of psychoanalysts, while the latter can be quite horrified at the methodological narrowness of the former.

A related difficulty in assessing studies of child development concerns testability. It is far from clear how many of the views about children can be tested and thereby possibly eliminated; and again the social and human sciences may be contrasted with the physical sciences, where a theory would be given no consideration at all unless some test of it was, at least, possible in principle. This was argued convincingly by Popper. A scientific theory can always be used to make accurate predictions, and this means that the theory is open to the possibility of refutation, for the prediction may turn out to be incorrect. Of course, if the prediction is substantiated, this does not mean that the theory is proven in any absolute sense, rather it has been confirmed by passing a serious test. Popper cited the example of Einstein's theory of relativity, which led to the prediction that certain anomalies would occur as a distant star passed behind the sun and was eclipsed. This seemingly unlikely prediction, which raised the possibility of refuting Einstein's theory, was confirmed by Eddington in 1919.[24] From this starting point, Popper proceeded to argue that because a theory can explain some phenomenon *after the fact* is not sufficient to qualify it as scientific. He cited Marxism and Freudian psychology as examples; these theories were not scientific, for they never faced the possibility of refutation. Whatever happened, whatever evidence turned up, these theories could *then* assimilate and explain. Theories that can explain everything and anything are perfectly safe and need never be abandoned; hence, they are not scientific.

Both these aspects of Popper's work are relevant to the discussion of theories of child development. Many of these theories purport to be scientific, and many appear to have great explanatory power. But it is not clear how they could be put to the test, or how their adherents could ever be persuaded to abandon them. Erikson's theory faces difficulties of this kind, although some experimental support for his theories has recently started to come in. However, many attacks have been made on Freudian psychology, some along the lines outlined by Popper, and if it is found to be unscientific, then the same verdict would seem to apply to Erikson's work, with its psychoanalytic foundations. Indeed, as has been seen in the foregoing discussion, some adherents of the analytic framework have argued that it is a mistake to regard psychoanalysis as science—it is a different enterprise, perhaps nearer to the humanities than the sciences.

Similar problems of testability and hence of refutation also arise in the case of Piaget's work. However, his theories would be unscientific only if they were untestable in principle; practical difficulties that hamper testing do not make a theory unscientific. There are many scientific theories that our present technology renders untestable but that are testable in principle, as, for example, some astronomical and cosmological theories. At this point the issue again becomes clouded. In the first place, it is not always evident whether a difficulty is a difficulty "in principle." Matters of theoretical principle and matters of fact are not clearly demarcated. Consider the making of predictions. From the fact that a child at a certain stage of development has certain characteristics, Piaget cannot scientifically predict what it will be like when it reaches maturity. Now, it is hard to say whether the difficulties in making this kind of prediction are practical difficulties, due to our present lack of facts and techniques, or whether they are difficulties in principle. Is it possible, even only in principle, to make certain kinds of prediction about the future? The schoolmaster in Dylan Thomas's "Return Journey" expressed the commonsense view:

> one finds it hard to reconcile one's memory of a small
> none-too-clean urchin lying his way unsuccessfully out of his
>   homework
> with a fierce and many-medalled sergeant-major with three
> children or a divorced chartered accountant;
> and it is hard to realize
> that some little tousled rebellious youth whose only claim
> to fame among his contemporaries was his undisputed right
> to the championship of the spitting contest
> is now perhaps one's own bank manager.[25]

The second difficulty with respect to the testability of Piaget's work is that a distinction has to be drawn between the facts Piaget discovered about children and the theories he erected upon this body of fact. Again this distinction is far from clear because, as was argued earlier, the facts are described in theoretical terms. The point, however, is that factual discoveries may result from work that is scientifically exemplary, but this does not automatically mean that associated theories will have the necessary characteristics to warrant their being classed as scientific. Piaget has done work that falls into both these distinct categories. The worth of each type of work must be judged separately, despite Piaget's and his expositors' refusal to make the separation. Some of his supporters even go so far as to criticize other researchers on the grounds that they are "merely empirical," and they eulogize Piaget's stages for transcending the empirical realm by providing "a theoretical taxonomy."[26]

Finally, Piaget's theories have certain built-in features that also militate against accurate prediction and hence against the possibility of refutation. Piaget recognized that certain aspects of a person's behavior may be at a higher level than other aspects, and he acknowledged that a child may occasionally get a certain type of problem right without consistently getting it right. In practice this means that it is always possible to explain an event after it has happened: the child should be able to solve a problem because he or she is at developmental stage X, but if he or she cannot solve it, then in this particular aspect of development that child is not at stage X, although the rest of its development is. Thus, whether the child can solve the problem or not, its behavior can be explained. Unfortunately, of course, there is a corresponding difficulty about making predictions.

Despite these difficulties, it is clear that Piaget's theories do take a stand in ruling out certain forms of behavior—some things are not possible for children to accomplish at certain stages. And, as mentioned earlier, some experimentalists have been able to devise tests that do suggest that, in some respects at least, Piaget's ideas are deficient. One example will suffice to illustrate the point. Piaget believed—as we have seen—that an infant did not know that physical objects are permanent, for when he hid something under the infant's blanket the baby would not search for it. But an alternative hypothesis is possible: perhaps infants have incompletely developed memories and, within a second or two, forget about the object that was hidden! Jerome Kagan has recently described some experiments that suggest this is a better explanation than Piaget's. Kagan concludes, "Many puzzling phenomena that appear during the last third of the first year become more understandable if we assume that the child's ability to retrieve the past and to hold it in active memory are being enhanced."[27]

§   §   §

THE questions that have been raised about studies of child growth come to a focus in the work of the best-known figure of all, Dr. Benjamin Spock, whose popular child-care handbook has sold thirty million copies (sales surpassed only by the Bible). What model did he adopt, and how did it influence what he observed in children? Is it relevant to evaluate his work using scientific criteria, or did it have some other purpose?

The charge that was often brought against Dr. Spock, and to which he finally pleaded "guilty" in 1974—of fostering permissiveness and hence spoiling a generation of children—tends to obscure the fact that in many ways he is an old-fashioned figure. This emerges clearly if one examines the outline of human development that appears in his handbook *Baby and Child Care*—an account that has been digested by millions of parents. In organizing his handbook, Spock adopted the orthodox division of growth into a number of convenient stages: infancy, the one-year-old, the two-year-old, from three to six, from six to eleven, and the onset of puberty. The infant was portrayed as needing love and attention as well as food and warmth, and although it was small, it was not necessarily frail and was able to make certain desires known. As Spock put it, "your baby is born to be a reasonable, friendly human being."[28] The one-year-old was seen by Spock as realizing "that he's a human being with ideas and a will of his own,"[29] as being compelled by his nature to assert himself, and as having a passion to explore. The two-year-old imitated adult behavior and might be quite dependent, but later might show signs of "balkiness and other inner tensions."[30] This behavior faded at three, and for the next few years, the child was warm and tender with a good deal of admiration for its parents. Subsequent stages of development were described, but the handbook's chief concern was with the younger child.

The theoretical views that color this account of child development are not difficult to detect. Apart from the influence of evolutionary theory (indicated by his dabbling with the theory of recapitulation), they fall into three main categories. In the first place, Spock relied heavily upon pediatric research in such fields as childhood diseases and infant nutrition. Second, he had a strong commitment to liberal political ideals, a commitment that eventually led to his involvement in the anti–Vietnam War movement in the United States and his trial in 1967 for conspiracy to violate the Selective Services Act. In *Baby and Child Care*, his political leanings revealed themselves in his stress on the rights of both baby and parents, for all members of the family are depicted as having rights, duties, and needs:

> Books about child care, like this one, put so much emphasis on all the needs that children have—for love, for understanding, for patience, for consistency, for firmness, for protection, for comradeship, for calories and vitamins—that parents sometimes feel physically and emotionally exhausted just from reading about what is expected of them. They get the impression that they are meant to have no needs themselves.[31]

Spock dispelled this impression in his chapter "The Parents' Part," where even his subheadings were revealing: "Parents Are Human," "They Have Needs," "Some Children Are More Difficult than Others," "At Best, There's Lots of Hard Work and Deprivation," "Needless Self-sacrifice Sours Everybody," and "Parents Should Expect Something from Their Children." The tenor of his discussion gives only a little support to the charge that he sponsored permissiveness.

Revising *Baby and Child Care* in 1957, over a decade after it first appeared, Spock admitted that "a lot has been added and changed, especially about discipline, spoiling and the parents' part,"[32] and he claimed that the original edition had led to some misunderstanding of his attempt to encourage the relaxing of the "fairly strict and inflexible" attitude toward child rearing that existed in the mid-1940s. When the revised edition was being prepared, the pendulum had swung the other way; the danger he now saw was that a conscientious parent might get "into trouble with permissiveness,"[33] so he attempted to counterbalance this. Later still, in *Decent and Indecent*, he admitted to being worried that "my own particular ideals and standards might seem so old-fashioned."[34]

A further major influence on Spock was psychoanalytic theory. In *Baby and Child Care*, his views on such matters as toilet training, feeding schedules, and general child management were based, as he put it, on the work of "educators, psychoanalysts, and pediatricians."[35] In *Decent and Indecent*, the psychoanalytic framework was even more apparent than it was in the handbook; in dealing with "Our Personal and Political Behavior," he covered such topics as the source of human idealism, problems of sex and sex role, aggression and hostility, the psychology of political attitudes, and the function of education. His basic thesis in all these discussions was stated simply:

> We mislead ourselves by assuming that the judgments and courses of action we come to are based on reasoning whereas they are often quite irrational and even self-defeating. Nevertheless, these deeper drives do follow patterns that have been analyzed and explained, first by Freud.[36]

In his writings, Spock was not always sufficiently aware of the important methodological distinction between classification and explanation. To fit a phenomenon into a classification, or to give it a name, is not necessarily to explain it, although it may induce a feeling of comfort in readers. Readers of his handbook are particularly likely to fall victims to this fallacy. The young baby cries for no apparent reason at a certain time each day; the parents are relieved to discover that it is a case of "periodic irritable crying." This bears comparison with the classic case in which a person suffering from a mysterious fever is comforted by the doctor's diagnosis of "pyrexia of unknown origin." Or, when a child suddenly develops a fear of water, it is because he or she is at the one-year stage of development. Sometimes the child becomes difficult to manage, he contradicts his parents, and he

> has a hard time making up his mind, and then he wants to change it. He acts like a person who feels he is being bossed too much, even when no one is bothering him. He is quite bossy himself. He insists on doing things just so, doing them his own way, doing them exactly as he has always done them before.[37]

The explanation is simple: "In the period between 2 and 3, children are apt to show signs of balkiness and other inner tensions. . . . It looks as though the child's nature between 2 and 3 is urging him to decide things for himself."

Obviously, these examples of classification are re-descriptions of the phenomena in different terminology, and classifying the phenomena in this way does not serve to explain them. But in fairness to Spock, it may be that he did not always intend this type of passage to masquerade as an explanation. Sometimes he may have been attempting to give a description of the typical behavior of children at different ages. Perhaps it is as well to end here by repeating a caution applicable to Dr. Spock and his forebears in the field of child study. Descriptions of typical behavior can only be made in the context of a theory, because what is to count as "typical behavior" very much depends upon the point of view of the observer, and furthermore, the language that is used to describe the behavior is usually borrowed from a theory, or may have political or ideological connotations. Thus, what the observer sees in children depends upon what model he or she brings along.

7.

AN UPBRINGING FIT FOR SOCIETY:
MARX AND DEWEY

THE nineteenth century was characterized in part by vigorous discussion of the relationship between the individual and society. The framework in which this took place was in large measure derived from the writings of Georg Wilhelm Friedrich Hegel, a German idealist philosopher whose work in the early nineteenth century asserted the primacy of society in the ordering of human conduct. This philosophical system had gradually grown in influence and spread from Germany to the English-speaking world. In Britain Hegel was popularized by the publication of J. H. Stirling's book *The Secret of Hegel*; it is a fair indication of the turgidity and impenetrability of Hegel's prose, and hence of his thought, that one commentator said Stirling had managed to keep the secret very well. Hegel is best known to modern readers for his theory of the dialectical process, according to which thought develops by means of contradiction and reconciliation; the progression is from a thesis, to the antithesis, and on to a temporary resting place in the synthesis, which soon becomes a second thesis and starts the cycle over.

Both Karl Marx and John Dewey, who were major influences on social thought in the twentieth century (including the fields of child rearing and education), owed Hegel a great debt. It is remarkable that two men who, in some respects, have become representatives of quite opposed ideologies, could have grown from the same intellectual roots. But, if ideology is cast aside and their works compared, many similarities emerge—not least being their similar concern to outline a schooling that was directly relevant to social living.

Marx was raised in Germany during a period when Hegel's influence was perhaps at its height; he later claimed to have thoroughly absorbed Hegel and to have seen that his predecessor's thought needed to be inverted in order to reveal its true insights.

> My dialectic method is not only different from the Hegelian, but is its direct opposite. . . . With him it is standing on its head. It must be turned right side up again, if you would discover the rational kernel within the mystical shell.[1]

Marx was referring to the fact that Hegel saw the dialectical process at work in the realm of ideas or spirit, whereas he saw it at work in the physical realm. Marx was proud of having put Hegel "on his feet."[2]

Dewey, on the other hand, was raised in New England at a time when there were close ties between American and German universities; he was introduced to Hegel by his professors, most of whom had done their graduate work in Europe. Dewey, too, was influenced by the dialectical method, which he renamed the method of resolution of "dualisms." Later in life, Dewey wrote, "I should never think of ignoring, much less denying, what an astute critic occasionally refers to as a novel discovery—that acquaintance with Hegel has left a permanent deposit in my thinking."[3]

The writings of both Marx and Dewey are voluminous. Marx wrote on economics, philosophy, history, literature, science, and political change; and Dewey wrote on an even broader set of topics (including, of course, a great deal on education). In an age before Xerox copiers and electronic word processors, Dewey wrote about forty books and eight hundred journal articles. Their works are too rich to summarize accurately in a brief space, but one underlying theme in both writers—which reflects an important theme in Hegel— is their concern with the way individuals are shaped to a profound degree by the society into which they are born. Hegel put the central notion as follows:

> Any merely particular action or business of the individual relates to the needs of himself as a natural being. But these, his commonest functions, are saved from nothingness and given reality solely by the universal maintaining medium, that is, through the power of the whole people of which he is a member. It is this power, too, which gives content as well as form to his actions. . . . The labor of the individual for his own wants is at the same time a satisfying of the needs of others, and reciprocally the satisfaction of his own needs is attained only through the labor of others.[4]

§   §   §

THIS insight into the importance of society provided a theoretical starting point for radical thinkers seeking improved working conditions, democracy, and a secular state. In 1827, the philanthropic businessman and social reformer Robert Owen coined the words "socialist" and "communist,"[5] and the terms were used interchangeably for many years. Marx came to socialism in 1843 by a circuitous route. Born in 1818 of Jewish parents who had converted to Protestantism, the young Marx attended a Jesuit–run secondary school for five years, where he was subject to strict discipline. As a university student, he ran up debts, duelled, and was arrested for "noisiness and drunkenness,"[6] before settling down to become one of the best-read scholars of his age.

Marx not only studied Hegel and his disciples but also the British philosophers Locke, Bentham, and Hume and Continental thinkers such as Voltaire, Rousseau, Helvétius, and Feuerbach. He read deeply in the Greek poets, the French classics, and Shakespeare —whom he learned by heart. Among those who impressed him was Darwin, and when he wrote *Capital*, Marx asked the evolutionary theorist if he could dedicate the work to him. Darwin, less than enthusiastic, politely evaded the offer by pointing out that he was no economist.[7] In 1841 Marx was granted a doctorate by Jena University.

In 1844 Marx began his lifelong collaboration with Friedrich Engels, whose knowledge of the business world and working-class life fleshed out many of Marx's arid economic arguments, and who added his own insights to the communist corpus. Engels helped support Marx financially, as well. The Engels family were prosperous mill owners engaged in the Rhineland cotton trade. As Protestant pietists, they gave their son a religious upbringing and taught him respect for the throne, neither attribute lasting long after he left home. Among the prolific Engels's earliest writings were tracts defending Hegel's mode of argument as distinct from his Absolutist speculations. From 1842 to 1844 Engels lived in England, where he had been sent by his family to learn English business procedures, and it was during this time that he collected material for *The Condition of the Working Class in England*, which included revelations on the abuse of children in the factory system. The coming together of the two young intellectuals was described by Marx as the beginning of "running a joint business."[8] When they constructed the proposition that economic factors were the major agency of social change, Marx was twenty-seven and Engels twenty-five.

§   §   §

FOR Marx, the existence of social groups such as families and institutions such as schools was best understood through an analysis of the economic base of society. If there are stages of development in production, commerce, or consumption, then there will be corresponding forms of social constitution, whether of the family or of the classes. In a word, there will be a corresponding civil society.[9]

The well-to-do family of Marx's and Engels's day appeared to be representative of the capitalist structure of society and seemed to enforce capitalism's bourgeois purposes. The family was based on property relations, dependence of the wife on the husband, and the existence of children who represented the family's economic interest through the inheritance of wealth. Were capitalism and private gain to be abolished, the bourgeois structure would collapse, and family affection based on real relationships would emerge.

As far as the working class was concerned, Marx and Engels were less interested in abstract structural analysis. They saw the factory system, which drew many women out of the home, as breaking down the family unit. According to Engels, the working wife's constant employment "unsexes the man and takes from the woman all womanliness."[10] Girls sent to work could learn nothing of keeping a household: they cannot "knit, sew, wash or cook . . . and when they have young children to take care of, have not the vaguest idea how to set about it."[11] They also learned an unhealthy independence: "A man berated his two daughters for going to the public house, and they answered that they were tired of being ordered about, saying, 'Damn you, we have to keep you.' " The two girls then left their father to starve.[12]

Marx's own life as head of a family was conventional, if an illegitimate son born to a faithful servant is excluded. Jenny Marx had seven children, and Karl was notably affectionate, playing games with them, "swopping" toys, and taking them on lengthy walks, telling long stories on the way. One of his sons-in-law described him as "a loving, gentle and indulgent father."[13] Marx also said he admired Jesus for his love of children. Nonetheless, the family suffered from his indigent circumstances. In the early 1850s Marx could not afford to call the doctor or pay for medicine, and the family lived on a diet of bread and potatoes. Jenny had to borrow from a friend to pay for one child's funeral. Of the three children who survived to adulthood, two (in unhappy marriages) would take their own lives. One biographer has said of Marx that he "sacrificed the life and health of his own."[14] Engels, by way of contrast, lived a secret life in the slums of Manchester with a red-haired Irish working-class woman.

The "social whole" conceptualized by Marx and Engels dealt equally with individuals, along with families and other social groups. As Marx explained:

> The state itself educates its members by . . . converting the aims of the individual into general aims, crude instinct into moral incli- nation, natural independence into spiritual freedom, by the indi- vidual finding his good in the life of the whole, and the whole in the frame of mind of the individual.[15]

His concept of the state assumed an association of free human beings who educate one another.[16] Marx, though, experienced little of this form of government personally—either in Germany, where his critical remarks led to government suppression of the newspaper that employed him, or in England, where he knew of the oppressive conditions of workers (many of whom were children and adolescents). Of all nations it was Britain that provided the "object lesson" for the Marxist analysis. Marx arrived in London in 1849, and it was to be his home for the rest of his life. When he came to write *Capital* in 1867, he noted his reliance on English example, claiming that this nation was the "classic ground" for the study of the capitalist mode of production and exchange.[17]

§   §   §

THE Industrial Revolution, as Marx observed it, was changing the class structure of Europe, and with it, the concept of childhood. Admittedly, children had worked for their families from time imme- morial, with a nonworking childhood being the prerogative of a small social elite. For most children, when they were old enough, it was dawn to dusk in the fields, or on-the-job training in the towns, or working at the myriad tasks of family life. Along with their mothers, children were the mainstay of the small domestic enterprises of weav- ing and spinning, which relied upon the cheapest of labor. It aroused little comment in 1796 when Prime Minister William Pitt pointed out to the English Parliament "how much could be done by the industry of children and how advantageous it was to employ them early."[18] Unique in the use of child labor in the early nineteenth century was the huge number of children marshalled for incessantly repetitive work under strict discipline by those with little or no regard for their well-being. Those who were worn out were discarded like any other piece of used machinery. The expansion of the cities (Bradford in

Yorkshire, for instance, grew from a population of 13,000 in 1801 to 104,000 in 1851[19]) ensured a pool of youthful workers, who became important for the profitability of British industry. In 1833, William Cobbett reported that Britain's national wealth, power, and security were dependent on the labor of 300,000 little girls in Lancashire.[20] The activities of this army of child laborers were reported on intermittently under Factory Acts legislation, which, if slow to amend abuses, at least made them increasingly visible.

The writings of Marx and Engels drew extensively on British government reports on child labor, which detailed the shocking abuse of children in early nineteenth-century Britain. The children of paupers were auctioned off or apprenticed at as young as three years of age, four- and five-year-olds opened and shut underground mining ventilation doors in twelve-hour shifts, and half-grown girls were harnessed to pull tubs of coal along mine shafts. Adolescent girls worked continuously, with only short breaks for sleep, without even time to undress. Some children even "worked" in their sleep. The men of the household were less concerned about their children working than their wives. "The wretched half-starved parents think of nothing but getting as much as possible out of their children."[21] Children were kept under the eye of unfeeling overseers who brought into the factory "the brutality which the standards of their time permitted them to practice on their wives and children at home."[22] Indeed, the overseers needed to get the quota of work done or they would face dismissal themselves. Runaways were beaten back to the mills and mines. Overall, the children were "worse slaves than the negroes in America, for they are more sharply watched."[23]

Marx and Engels hypothesized that the introduction of machines devalued the work of men and enhanced that of women and children, who were cheaper to employ. Skilled workers were replaced by the unskilled, men by women, and adults by children. One man's wage would pay for the employment of a woman and three children: "*four times* as many lives are used up to earn the livelihood for *one* worker's family."[24] Men, women, and children became "instruments of labour, more or less expensive to use, according to their age and sex."[25] Working hours were increased and wages were reduced. In sum, the British factory system destroyed the working man's independence, dissolved his family, and divided society into the "great capitalists" and the "non-possessing workers."[26]

The physical effects of the work regimen on young children were horrendous. Marx described it as "making money out of the marrow and blood of women and children."[27] The English reformer Lord Shaftesbury put the case poignantly when he described a group of factory children: "They seemed to me, such were their crooked shapes, like a mass of crooked alphabets."[28] Nineteen-year-olds looked like eleven-year-olds; children were deformed and scrofulous; and tuberculosis was rampant. In 1833, a doctor noted conditions in his town:

> The boys and girls whom I examined from the Manchester factories very generally exhibited a depressed look, and a pallid complexion; none of the alacrity, activity, and hilarity of early life shone in their countenances and gestures.[29]

He feared the English were turning into a race of pygmies.

Many children were crippled or died through industrial accidents. "The industrial bulletin of the factory inspectors is more terrible and appalling than any of the war bulletins from the Crimea."[30] One group of owners was fined 298 pounds for 18 deaths and 1,770 mutilations—"less than the cost of a third class racehorse."[31] It was declared that "the fate of the slaves in the worst of the American plantations was golden in comparison with that of the English workers in that period."[32] In the opinion of Engels, communism must come to pass because "communism is a question of humanity."[33]

Nineteenth-century children, in the words of the poet Shelley, were "being turned into lifeless, bloodless machines at an age when they should have been at play."[34] There were, of course, apologists aplenty for the factory system. It was necessary to create a disciplined labor force; managers were entitled to conduct their own businesses; no one had a right to interfere with an Englishman's liberties. Cases of enlightened owners and friendly overseers were cited. Andrew Ure reported that "the work of these lively elves seemed to resemble a sport."[35] Another observer noted that the children "seemed to be always cheerful and alert, taking pleasure in the light play of their muscles, enjoying the mobility natural to their age."[36] They showed no traces of exhaustion at all! The Leeds *Mercury* confidently predicted that no child could suffer injury from working a mere eleven hour day.[37] Children were said to enjoy the steamy warmth of the factory, and showed great keenness in improving themselves at Sunday School on their day off.

It took nearly a century to convince the British public that a working-class childhood should not replicate a working-class adulthood. By the second half of the nineteenth century, the Factory Acts were curbing the most blatant abuses. Social reformers, politically and religiously motivated, contributed to changing attitudes by challenging the dictum that poverty and pauperism were necessary concommitants of industrialization and private and public wealth. There is even modern evidence (which Marx would have appreciated) that conditions changed partly because child labor became increasingly less economically attractive. Whatever the reasons for change, that the abuses of a working childhood were acceptable for so long despite their public discussion is testimony to the strength of entrenched practices.

§   §   §

THE later British Factory Acts required some schooling for child workers. However, the regulations were frequently evaded or the education that was provided was worse than useless. Teachers were "worn out workers,"[38] some of whom could not even spell their own names, and there was little or no supervision.

Children were frequently too tired and slept on their benches in the factory classrooms. Regular school attendance fell as factories multiplied. Engels reported the case of a boy of seventeen who "did not know how many two and two made,"[39] and of a girl who attended school and Sunday School who had "never learnt of another world, nor of heaven, nor of another life."[40] Less surprisingly, the children knew of the exploits of the highwayman Dick Turpin and of the thief and jailbreaker Jack Sheppard. In 1859, Marx made the telling point: "In fact, the educational clauses of the Factory Acts, while they require children to have certificates of school attendance, do not require that they have learned anything."[41]

Speaking generally, Marx and Engels regarded education as a process that served the ruling class by indoctrinating the masses with the dominant ideas of the day. It was a subordinate activity of humans, for social change was the product of class struggle and revolution rather than education. Nonetheless, a socialist education would be important in helping modify the economic base of society, enlightening the masses, and ensuring their adherence to communist policy. The two men believed in comprehensive, nonalienating schooling taking place in a communal situation that would enable the child to unfold its talents. Marx and Engels had little regard for forms of schooling under church and bourgeois control, which they felt served the interests of the capitalist state.

The process of capitalist education was seen as separating the noble, wise, and articulate from the silent, inarticulate, and oppressed. "Society wrongs individuals twice over when it makes ignorance a necessary consequence of poverty,"[42]—a thought shared by American participants in the "War on Poverty" a century later. Education should be free, secular, and compulsory; this would ensure the untrammeled exercise of the national intellect and the flowering of science, thus paving the way to social salvation. Society gained more from the educated than from the ignorant and uncultivated; only when a society was educated could calm and peaceful social change occur. Marx quoted French political philosopher Montesquieu on the form education should take: "The state must see to it that everybody receives sufficient education to be able to learn something useful in the world."[43] By "useful," Marx did not mean "filling up exercise books which can make a student dull witted in six months,"[44] or "the ledger, the desk and business" for boys, or the polite "accomplishments" for girls, but rather "the real education of the mind."[45]

§   §   §

GRANTED that the child was part of society, and that society demanded that its members earn their livings when fit to do so, it followed that communist education should have a work component. Marx had read the writings of the social utopians—Fourier, Saint-Simon, and Cabet— whose never-never lands of planned happiness included organized schemes for education. Also among this group was Robert Owen, who both preached and practiced new forms of social activity, including the reform of schools in New Lanark, the model mill town that he managed at the end of the eighteenth century. Owen was also aware of the communitarian experiments of the American Shakers, with their principle of "combined labour and expenditure."[46] Marx specifically mentioned Owen when discussing his own educational ideas in *Capital*.

Owen argued that a person's behavior was fashioned primarily by the environment and that this environment could take on any required character "by the application of proper means."[47] With the happiness of the community would come the happiness of the self. The "application of proper means" was equated with education. Good traits, Owen believed, were best implanted early, for "much of the good or evil is taught to and acquired by a child at a very early period of its life."[48] He wanted infant schools where children could be protected from their untaught parents and brought up in favorable surroundings as soon as they could walk. Teachers must never beat or threaten children, should always display a pleasant countenance and kind manner, and should teach the laws of nature through things rather than books. Here Owen was echoing the advice of Rousseau. A night school was also established at New Lanark where parents could be transformed into rational creatures. Such rationality was impossible to learn, Owen believed, in the highly regulated monitorial school system of his day, which demanded extremes of obedience and docility. Owen told his fellow manufacturers that if they improved the lot of their "living machines,"[49] they would raise their profits, and that if they did not mend their own fences, the state would undertake the task for them.

Marx was more than skeptical of most of the utopian educators, declaring that they may have had revolutionary ideas at the beginning but that their followers created reactionary sects that merely *dreamed* of realization. Such educational plans deserved constant evaluation. "Is not education itself also human and therefore imperfect? Does not education itself also require education?"[50]

Marx and Engels attempted to relate education and work through the concept of productive labor, or "polytechnical education," as it became known. Codicil 10 of the *Communist Manifesto* of 1848 proclaimed the "abolition of child factory labour in its present form. Combination of education with industrial production." This proposition was further expanded in *Capital*, where Marx noted that the 1864 Factory Act made the provision of elementary education an indispensable condition for the employment of children. Marx believed that the success of the Act's educational clauses proved the possibility of combining education and gymnastics (drill in the case of boys) with manual labor. The Factory Act inspectors argued that although working children received only half the education of regular day scholars, they learned quite as much and often more. "The system on which they work, half manual labour, and half school, renders each employment a rest and a relief to the other";[51] whereas the teacher of the more privileged children of the upper and middle classes, who sets his charges to long monotonous hours of study, "wastes the time, health, and energy of the children."[52] Marx summed up:

> From the Factory system budded, as Robert Owen has shown us
> in detail, the germ of the education of the future, an education
> that will, in the case of every child over a given age, combine

productive labour with instruction and gynmastics, not only as one of the methods of adding to the efficiency of production, but as the only method of producing fully developed human beings.[53]

The concept of productive labor became part of the ethos of communist education, with an understanding and valuation of work regarded as essential to a rounded education. Marx died in 1883 largely unaware of the vitality of the intellectual seeds he had sown. His remarks on productive labor were taken up with great seriousness in the USSR in the 1920s and in the People's Republic of China fifty years later. Both nations attempted a range of activities in efforts to embody Marxist principles as they understood them. For all that, Marx remained true to his Hegelian past, holding that any particular form of education was subsumed within a greater social whole. It was, in Marx's view, childish and stupid merely to reduce society's ills to neglected education.

§   §   §

JOHN DEWEY was born in 1859, the year in which Darwin's *Origin* also first saw the light of day, and he lived for almost a century, dying in 1952. As a philosopher, he was a leading exponent of pragmatism, and recent scholars have judged him to be one of the major thinkers of the modern era.[54] For a number of years around the turn of the century he was chairman, at the University of Chicago, of an unusual department—philosophy, psychology, and education were melded together. Dewey wrote in all three areas, and he took an active interest in the Laboratory School that was associated with his department (and which is still in existence). He was also heavily involved in the social and political issues of his age, both nationally and internationally. He was among those vitally interested in experiments in productive labor in communist countries. While Dewey opposed what he regarded as "the stereotyped formulae of Marxian philosophy,"[55] he closely followed the educational reforms of the early communist regime in Russia, which involved dovetailing schoolwork with out-of-school social activities. He was troubled also by conditions in the United States in inner cities and so was active in the "settlement house" movement, which set up houses as types of community centers in depressed areas. He became a leader of the "progressive movement," which started as a general social reform movement but quickly came to focus upon educational change as a practical way of improving society.[56] His influential thought about education, which was forged basically in the years at Chicago, reflected three major influences. In the preface to his major work, *Democracy and Education* (1916), Dewey wrote:

> The philosophy stated in this book connects the growth of democracy with the development of the experimental method in the sciences, evolutionary ideas in the biological sciences, and the industrial reorganization, and is concerned to point out the changes in subject matter and method of education indicated by these developments.[57]

Inspired directly by Hegel's dialectical method, Dewey approached almost every problem by identifying the dualisms or opposing viewpoints that existed and then mounting an argument to show that both views had some truth-content but that an adequate solution was to be found only in the amalgamation of the two. (In other words, he tried to achieve an Hegelian "synthesis" between a "thesis" and its "antithesis.")

During a visit to the USSR in 1928, Dewey had been as impressed by its child colonies for orphans and refugees, and by its lively school projects, as he was depressed by the sterility of Marxist dogmas. His expectation was that the Russian schools would leaven the Marxist philosophical lump. Typically, he expressed his ideas in the language of the dialectic:

> It seems impossible that an education intellectually free will not militate against a servile acceptance of dogma as dogma. One hears all the time about a dialectic movement by means of which a movement contradicts itself in the end. I think the schools are a "dialectic" factor in the evolution of Russian communism.[58]

In *Democracy and Education* he resolved more than thirty dualisms in his typical fashion. The titles of many of his books also reflected this method of approach: *The School and Society, The Child and the Curriculum, Interest and Effort in Education, Experience and Nature*, and so forth. Thus, in *The Child and the Curriculum*, Dewey was concerned with the issue of whether the child and its interests should be the dominant concern in education, or whether the focus should be on the bodies of knowledge (the curriculum) that had to be imparted to the child. The opening portion of the book outlined these opposing viewpoints, and Dewey showed that, taken separately, each had some merit. But the only way to avoid their defects was to see that there really was no opposition—the curriculum of schools has developed, historically, *from* human interests. So it is quite possible to interest the child in the bodies of knowledge in the curriculum, providing the teacher (using his or her knowledge of psychology) leads the child to explore them in fruitful ways—a nice Hegelian synthesis.

Dewey was at his most Hegelian in the first half of his long life, and, reflecting the passage from Hegel quoted at the beginning of the present chapter, he believed that an individual must be seen as a member of a social group, for without the group the individual was nothing. He rejected the dualism that raised the question "Which is more important, the individual or society?" He wrote in 1897:

> In sum, I believe that the individual who is to be educated is a social individual, and that society is an organic union of individuals. If we eliminate the social factor from the child we are left only with an abstraction; if we eliminate the individual factor from society, we are left only with an inert and lifeless mass.[59]

While society could not survive without the contribution of the individual, the individual without the influence of society would be nothing short of bestial. Rousseau had wanted Emile to admire Robinson Crusoe, for the shipwrecked adventurer was the epitome of a resourceful individual living in a state of nature far from the corrupting influence of society; but Dewey would have stressed that Crusoe was only able to survive, and keep his sanity, by the vestiges of society that he had with him on his island—his language, his hunting and farming and building skills, and his civilized habits. What little empirical evidence is available (even the case of the marooned Alexander Selkirk, upon which the story of Crusoe was based) seems to support Dewey's position.

Dewey made this same point in essays on a variety of topics; for example, when discussing the rugged individualists who were carving out empires as militant capitalists in the business world, he argued that

> there is not a single process involved in the production and distribution of goods that is not dependent upon the utilization of results which are the consequences of the method of collective, organic intelligence working in mathematics, physics and chemistry.[60]

Even when they are flying in the face of society, individuals are dependent upon socially determined skills and resources.

Hegel may have appealed to Dewey, in part, for a personal reason. Evidently he had vivid memories of his own early childhood at about the time of the outbreak of the Civil War, and he held a somewhat romanticized view of how, in small rural communities, even the most rugged individualist pitched in to help the group survive, for instance, over the fierce winter period. If candles were not made, if firewood was not gathered, life would be hard indeed. Individuals learned the elements of morality and discipline, and such things as the importance of doing a job well, from this sort of shared experience. "We cannot overlook the factors of discipline and of character building involved in this kind of life," Dewey wrote; it provided "training in habits of order and of industry, and in the idea of responsibility, of obligation to do something, to produce something, in the world."[61]

Dewey's words conjure up a notion of productive labor that is similar to the one that was dear to the hearts of Marx and Engels. Indeed, Dewey had noted the increasing interest of progressive educators in the United States of the 1920s in socially useful schooling:

> For a leading principle of this advanced doctrine was that participation in productive work is the chief stimulus and guide to self educative activity on the part of pupils, since such productive work is both in accord with the natural or psychological process of learning; and also provides the most direct road to connecting the school with social life.[62]

There is an interesting set of similarities and contrasts here, too, with the communal education of the Israeli kibbutzim.[63]

§　　　　§　　　　§

DEWEY applied this insight to education in an interesting way that has touched the lives of several generations of Americans. He realized that society had undergone rapid change, largely as a result of industrialization made possible by advances in science. The old days were gone forever, but no institutions had taken over responsibility for teaching children the important social lessons they would formerly have learned as a consequence of the now vanishing household and community structure. Where could the individual learn the lessons that once were imparted in the community itself? Presumably the answer is, "In the school." But Dewey recognized one serious problem—the school of his day was not fitted to teach such lessons effectively. The curriculum was centuries out of date, teaching practices were antediluvian, and even the physical layout of classrooms and schools was antiquated:

> Just as the biologist can take a bone or two and reconstruct the whole animal, so, if we put before the mind's eye the ordinary schoolroom, with its rows of ugly desks placed in geometrical order, crowded together so that there shall be as little moving room as possible . . . and add a table, some chairs, the bare walls, and possibly a few pictures, we can reconstruct the only educational activity that can possibly go on in such a place. It is all made "for listening."[64]

John Wesley, of course, would have seen nothing wrong with such a schoolroom, but Dewey was incensed. He became the leading advocate of educational reform; and some of his thinking about the lines along which schools should move closely paralleled ideas held by Hegel's Marxist descendants. In the first place, Dewey, like Rousseau and Piaget, saw that learning and activity went hand in hand. Children entrapped in tiny desks could listen, but they could not learn or think in any important sense of these terms. Mind had evolved in the human species in order to guide daily activities and thus to aid survival (a nice Darwinian argument Dewey acquired from William James), but in schools it was not allowed to fulfill this natural function. "The very word pupil," Dewey pointed out, "has almost come to mean one who is engaged not in having fruitful experiences. . . . Something which is called mind or consciousness is severed from the physical organs of activity."[65] He added that activity was generally regarded in the schools of his day as "an irrelevant and intruding physical factor." He went so far as to discuss the design of an adequate school—tables instead of desks, room to move and work, with laboratory and library areas near at hand. He foresaw, in other words, the modern elementary schoolroom. He even argued that the climate in school should resemble that found in the ideal family, where the parents talked with the child, encouraged its explorations, provided a warm and pleasant environment for it to read and paint and play in, and took it on stimulating excursions.

> Now, if we organize and generalize all of this, we have the ideal school. There is no mystery about it. . . . It is simply a question of doing systematically and in a large, intelligent, and competent way what for various reasons can be done in most households only in a comparatively meager and haphazard manner.[66]

Turning to the *content* of schooling, Dewey was particularly concerned that in the classrooms he was criticizing there was almost no social interaction between children; they never engaged in some joint task of great relevance to them that they could complete only by cooperative activity. So Dewey advocated introducing "occupations" into the classroom—the sort of activities that in bygone days children would have engaged in at home and in the local community, and which were so educative. Cooking, spinning, woodworking, and weaving were among his favorites. The school would become "a miniature community, an embryonic society."[67] Dewey's vision was noble:

> When the school introduces and trains each child of society into membership within such a little community, saturating him with the spirit of service, and providing him with the instruments of effective self-direction, we shall have the deepest and best guaranty of a larger society which is worthy, lovely, and harmonious.[68]

Dewey argued that the main reason "the present school cannot organize itself as a natural social unit is because this element of common and productive activity is absent."[69] Some of his readers misunderstood and thought Dewey wanted all children to learn a trade, but of course this was far from his intent. He wanted children to learn the social virtues of cooperation, consideration, the dignity of labor, concentration, workmanship, and so on, via firsthand experience. He also thought such occupations were of great intrinsic interest to children; furthermore, they provided a vehicle by which to interest children in history and science (he discussed how spinning could lead children to inquire into the invention of the "spinning jenny," and why cotton was much slower than wool in becoming commercially important). In contemporary Russia and China, somewhat similar ideas have influenced the conduct of schooling; there may even be a historical link, as Dewey visited both countries in the 1920s.

Dewey did not use one term that was important in contemporary Marxist writings about life in industrialized countries, namely "alienation," but he seems to have been aware of the problem, and he devised a solution that was not so far removed from the one favored by these more radical writers. Dewey did not want occupations taught in schools in such a way that children were trapped into them as future careers. The point of using them, as indicated earlier, was educational. Properly used, school occupations would give students a sense of the social role that these played, their impact on people's lives, and so forth. This "right educational use" would give those who engage in industrial callings desire and ability to share in social control, and ability to become masters of their industrial fate. It would enable them to saturate with meaning the technical and mechanical features which are so marked a feature of our machine system of production and distribution.[70]

It is easy, with hindsight, to see how, in the hurly-burly of daily life in schools, Dewey's ideas could be misapplied. Carefully disciplined activity became, in the worst settings, mere random movement; starting with the interests of children in order to lead into the established disciplines became, too often, a full-time quest for sugar-coating. Progressive education started to degenerate, and in the late 1950s it was parodied in a well-known cartoon that depicted a small child looking wistfully at the teacher and asking, "Do we really have to do what we want to again today?" Finally, the Russians launched the first artificial satellite, Sputnik, and a shocked United States blamed the state of its education for the fact that it had been beaten in the race to reach outer space. For a while "Deweyan" and "progressive" almost became terms of derision. A more balanced judgment is possible now; clearly Dewey's ideas did not fail, for they were never properly implemented. It can be argued that he completed the Rousseauean revolution—he liberated the child, but in a more disciplined and reasoned way than that advocated by his Swiss predecessor.

8.

THE CONDITIONED CHILD

THE work of Freud, Marx and Dewey, and of members of the child-study movement were not the only sources of new models of the child in the early decades of the twentieth century. In the mid-1920s John B. Watson's *Behaviorism* was published, drawing reviews claiming that it was perhaps "the most important book ever written" and that it marked "an epoch in the intellectual history of man."[1] Although the reviewers were taken by storm, members of the American Psychological Association had been given advance warning by a journal article Watson published in 1913, and had been sufficiently influenced to vote him into their presidency in 1915. Watson had also written other books that were less polemical, but clear enough in the general line taken.

From the beginning, the behaviorist revolution had opponents both inside psychology's ranks and out. Aldous Huxley satirized the possibilities of behavioral science in *Brave New World* (1932): babies mass-produced from bottled embryos, conditioned to have the attitudes that the leaders of society deemed fit, and held in sway by artificially stunted or developed intelligence and instilled fears. In one passage, certain to have had an impact on parents and teachers, Huxley described how eight-month-old babies were introduced to flowers and books—a passage apparently based on an actual experiment of Watson's. In Huxley's nursery, the babies crawled toward inviting books and flowers; when they reached them "there was a violent explosion. Shriller and ever shriller, a siren shrieked. Alarm bells maddeningly sounded."[2] Mild electric shocks followed:

> Books and loud noises, flowers and electric shocks—already in
> the infant mind these couples were compromisingly linked; and

after two hundred repetitions of the same or a similar lesson would be wedded indissolubly. What man has joined, nature is powerless to put asunder.[3]

Of course, Watson had not gone this far. All he had done was strike an iron bar with a steel hammer behind baby Albert every time a white rat was released near him. Albert ended by being frightened of a great many white objects, even of white Santa Claus whiskers.[4] Unfortunately, perhaps, he was removed from Watson's ambit before he could be "unconditioned."

Huxley was not concerned with challenging the effectiveness of Watson's methods. Rather, *Brave New World* was a literary plea that man be allowed to remain free. It was an account of the totalitarian conditions that could be brought about by the application of Watsonian techniques. Huxley made this clear in his foreword:

There is, of course, no reason why the new totalitarianism should resemble the old. . . . A really efficient totalitarian state would be one in which the all-powerful executive of political bosses and their army of managers control a population of slaves who do not have to be coerced, because they love their servitude. To make them love it is the task assigned, in present-day totalitarian states, to ministries of propaganda, newspaper editors, and school-teachers. But their methods are still crude and unscientific.[5]

This objection to behaviorism is a perennial one, and Watson (followed by B. F. Skinner) just as persistently countered it: random or accidental conditioning is ever present, and mankind would be better off if it were replaced by conditioning that is planned and under social control. In this way the human race could be perfected; irrational or disruptive attitudes could be replaced by ones that are socially useful. In this utopian view, the rearing of children is all-important, and behaviorists offered a new model of the processes involved:

Behaviorism ought to be a science that prepares men and women for understanding the principles of their own behavior. It ought to make men and women eager to rearrange their own lives, and especially eager to prepare themselves to bring up their own children in a healthy way. I wish I could picture for you what a rich and wonderful individual we should make of every healthy child if only we could let it shape itself properly and then provide for it a universe in which it could exercise that organization.[6]

This vision prompted one reviewer to comment, "One stands for an instant blinded with great hope."

§   §   §

THE model of childhood developed by Watson, and so strongly objected to by Huxley and others, was based on elements that, taken by themselves, actually had much to recommend them. One foundation of the model is indicated by the oft-repeated remark that behaviorism reduces man to the level of pigeons and rats. This was frankly admitted by Watson, and he made a convincing case that this was no weakness, but instead, one of behaviorism's strongest features.

For much of its history, psychology had been closely connected to philosophy, as the earlier discussion of John Locke bears witness. Around the 1870s, psychology clearly emerged as a separate field of study; however, introspection remained a key method used, even in the laboratories of the leading German experimental psychologists.[7] Psychology was described as the science of mental life, and the only access the experimenter seemed to have to this mental life was by way of introspection—personal observation directed at the realm of one's own "inner experience." The difficulty was that although this method produced some measure of agreement about the facts of "mental life," there were cases where skilled introspectionists seriously disagreed in their conclusions. Watson, realizing that a key to advance in physical science had been the objectivity of its data, which allowed general agreement to be reached among researchers, was highly critical of introspection:

> I do not wish unduly to criticize psychology. It has failed signally, I believe, during the fifty-odd years of its existence as an experimental discipline to make its place in the world as an undisputed natural science. . . . The time seems to have come when psychology must discard all reference to consciousness; when it need no longer delude itself into thinking that it is making mental states the object of observation.[8]

Unless introspection was abandoned, he stated, another two hundred years would still see the disputes unsettled.

If introspection had to go, what could replace it? Watson turned to a field where he himself had been working for a number of years, namely, animal psychology. From the vantage point of the last decades of the twentieth century, it seems obvious that there is much to be gleaned about ourselves from a study of animal behavior, though just how much remains a matter of dispute; and it sometimes comes as a shock to realize that this approach to psychology is only a little over a century old. Before 1859 the conventional view was that there was an unbridgeable gulf separating humans from the animals: humans possess a soul, whereas animals are automata or, at the very best, conscious automata.[9] The study of animals, therefore, could contribute nothing to an understanding of humans. But after the publication of Darwin's *Origin*, mankind was seen as biologically continuous with the brutes; humans were merely the highest members yet to have evolved within the animal kingdom. It was only because he lived after 1859 that Watson could have written:

> Psychology as the behaviorist views it is a purely objective experimental branch of natural science. Its theoretical goal is the prediction and control of behavior. . . . The behaviorist, in his efforts to get a unitary scheme of animal response, recognizes no dividing line between man and brute.[10]

Much of the work on animal intelligence immediately after Darwin was poor in quality as it was heavily anecdotal and anthropomorphic. George Romanes, for instance, reprinted stories he had collected about the incredible, almost human behavior of family pets. It was not until 1894 that Lloyd Morgan completed the Darwinian revolution in animal psychology by advocating the methodological rule or "law of parsimony" that has become known as "Lloyd Morgan's Canon": an animal's behavior must not be interpreted as the outcome of a higher mental process, reasoning or willing, for example, if it can be interpreted in terms of a lower mental process such as reflex, or instinct.[11]

This was the approach advocated by Watson. Psychology could advance only by limiting itself to what was observable, in the manner adopted by researchers who studied animals. What was observable, of course, was behavior. In Watson's words:

> I suppose I must confess to a deep bias on these questions. I have devoted nearly twelve years to experimentation on animals. It is natural that such a one should drift into a theoretical position which is in harmony with his experimental work. . . . What we need to do is to start work upon psychology, making behavior, not consciousness, the objective point of our attack.[12]

To Watson, an organism was situated in an environment, and the environmental conditions affecting its behavior were discoverable. But there was an important corollary: because the behavior of the organism was stimulated by factors in the environment, the possibility arose that by controlling these factors the psychologist could control behavior. This possibility was illustrated many years after Watson's original work by B. F. Skinner, who wrote an entertaining article for a popular science periodical on how to train any animal, or even a child, to do virtually anything by careful environmental control.[13]

It is possible to control the behavior of pets in this way because animal behavior has been the subject of close observation, but Watson knew this was not true of children to the same degree. In a small book on child care published in 1928, which was dedicated to "the first mother who brings up a happy child," he stated:

> Will you believe the almost astounding truth that no well-trained man or woman has ever watched the complete and daily development of a single child from its birth to its third year? Plants and animals we know about because we have studied them, but the human child, until very recently, has been a mystery.[14]

Although this was hard on Tiedemann and others, it made a defensible point.

The foregoing references to the control of behavior point to another major factor that influenced Watson's model of the child, namely, a philosophy of strict determinism. In the course of Western intellectual history there has been a perennial debate between those who claim that humans have free will and those who deny it by claiming that actions are completely determined by outside forces. This issue is particularly likely to arise in the course of philosophical and psychological investigations; the philosopher and psychologist William James was so disturbed by it that at one time he feared for his own sanity. James finally concluded that because he was free to choose sides, belief in free will was justified.[15] A similar concern with the issue of free will was evinced by Aldous Huxley in *Brave New World*. In one emotional scene, the Savage, who is not a product of the new scientific society, attempts to awaken some of the conditioned citizens to their true situation:

> "But do you like being slaves?" the Savage was saying as they entered the Hospital. His face was flushed, his eyes bright with ardour and indignation. "Do you like being babies? Yes, babies. Mewling and puking," he added, exasperated by their bestial

stupidity into throwing insults at those he had come to save. . . .
"Yes, puking!" he fairly shouted. Grief and remorse, compassion
and duty—all were forgotten now and, as it were, absorbed into
an intense overpowering hatred of these less than human monsters. "Don't you even understand what manhood and freedom
are?"[16]

Philosophically, of course, Huxley did not have a case. For if determinism is true, then the Savage's actions are as much causally determined as those of the "human monsters" he was trying to awaken.
Huxley did not provide any argument against this view.

Watson belonged to the rival camp; only a determinist can hope
to control behavior by controlling the environmental factors that elicit
it. In one passage from *Behaviorism*, after a discussion of two "mechanically determined" entities, a Ford and a Rolls Royce, he went on to
argue:

> Whence come these differences in the machine? In the case of
> man, all healthy individuals . . . start out *equal*. Quite similar
> words appear in our far-famed Declaration of Independence. The
> signers of that document were nearer right than one might expect,
> considering their dense ignorance of psychology. They would
> have been strictly accurate had the clause "at birth" been inserted
> after the word equal. It is what happens to individuals after birth
> that makes one a hewer of wood and a drawer of water, another
> a diplomat, a thief, a successful business man or a far-famed
> scientist. What our advocates of freedom in 1776 took no account
> of is the fact that the Deity himself could not equalize 40-year-
> old individuals who have had such different environmental train-
> ings as the American people have had.[17]

There is some similarity to the Lockean position discussed earlier; and in the light of Watson's example it is interesting to note that
Locke's ideas formed part of the foundation upon which those who
framed the Declaration of Independence had worked. Locke, too, held
to a form of determinism: humans are born equal in that they are
"blank tablets" equally open to sense experience, and it was the subsequent course of this experience that was responsible for at least
"nine parts in ten" of what they later became. But some post-Lockeans
were optimistic enough to think, in opposition to Watson's view, that
even forty-year-old individuals who were dissimilar because of their
past histories of experience could be reeducated to "think and feel
alike." On the other hand, it is Watson who must be regarded as

optimistic for writing: "Give me a dozen healthy infants, well-formed, and my own specified world to bring them up in and I'll guarantee to take any one at random and train him to become any type of specialist I might select."[18] Watson denied that heredity had any great impact, although it would not have been incompatible with determinism to acknowledge this as a source of influence.

Watson's determinism came out strongly in his book on child care. Most mothers, he claimed, believed that both the good and the bad features of their children were due to the "unfolding" of inborn characteristics. Watson, however, sensed the dawn of a "social Renaissance":

> This awakening is beginning to show itself in mothers who ask themselves this question: "Am I not almost wholly responsible for the way my child grows up? Isn't it just possible that almost nothing is given in heredity and that practically the whole course of development of the child is due to the way I raise it?" When she first faces this thought, she shies away from it as being too horrible.[19]

Watson argued that the environment provided by the parents, including the way they rewarded and punished the child, determined the subsequent development of behavior. Some Watsonian variations on this theme must have shocked his readers. He attacked the family as a social institution and expressed a preference for child rearing in institutions where there "are undoubtedly much more scientific ways of bringing up children, which will probably mean finer and happier children."[20] He pointed out that couples often give more thought to buying a car or a pet than to having a baby, and he stated categorically that "no mother has a right to have a child who cannot give it a room to itself for the first two years of infancy."[21] He also outlined experimental work that had led him to the conclusion that in the baby "there are no instincts. We build in at an early age everything that is later to appear."[22] He went on to apply this credo to a really controversial topic:

> How about its loves—its affectionate behavior? Isn't that "natural"? Do you mean to say the child doesn't *instinctively* love its mother? Only one thing will bring out a love response in the child—stroking and touching its skin, lips, sex organs, and the like. It doesn't matter at first who strokes it. It will "love" the stroker. This is the clay out of which all love—maternal, paternal, wifely, or husbandly—is made. Hard to believe? But true.[23]

Watson then launched into the dangers of kissing children, calling on the mothers of America to hold themselves back in the interests of child health—a theme with which he hit the newspaper headlines. Instead of kissing, which later produced individuals who were "totally unable to cope with the world,"[24] Watson proposed a substitute:

> There is a sensible way of treating children. Treat them as though they were young adults. Dress them, bathe them with care and circumspection. Let your behavior always be objective and kindly firm. Never hug and kiss them, never let them sit in your lap. If you must, kiss them once on the forehead when they say good-night. Shake hands with them in the morning.[25]

§   §   §

IN discussing the way in which childish fears of the dark and so on were "built in" by the parents, Watson introduced another important foundation of the behaviorist model of the child: "We have a name in the laboratory for fears built up in this experimental way. We call them conditioned fears, and we mean by that 'home-made' fears."[26] Just as Locke's determinism was associated with a psychological mechanism—in his case, the origin of ideas in experience and the association of ideas to produce complex groupings—so it was with Watson. The mechanism he selected was the one identified by Ivan Pavlov, namely, conditioning.

Here, Watson had a strange blind spot which becomes apparent when his work is contrasted with that of his contemporary E. L. Thorndike, who had also approached human psychology by way of experimental work on animals. Thorndike had formulated a law of learning, the so-called "law of effect." In brief, Thorndike had imprisoned cats in boxes having internal catches. If a cat managed to escape by accidentally releasing the catch, Thorndike gave it a morsel of food before reentombing it. He found that the cats eventually mastered the art of releasing themselves quickly.[27] He later generalized this in his law by holding that any act in a given situation (escaping from the box) that produces satisfaction (the rewarding morsel) becomes associated with that situation (the box) and is more likely to recur when the situation recurs. Or in short, an act having a satisfactory effect is likely to recur.

Watson never accepted the law of effect, and he failed to see that parts of Pavlov's work on conditioning pointed in the same direction. It was left to Clark L. Hull and Kenneth Spence, and even more to B. F. Skinner, to develop this untapped potential. Watson remained content to make use of Pavlov's work on "classical conditioning." As Watson explained it:

> Suppose for example we take an already established (unlearned) reaction with both stimulus and response known, such as:
>
> S ————————————————————————————▶ R
> Electric shock   Withdrawal of hand
>
> Now the mere visual stimulus of a patch of red light will not cause the withdrawal of the hand. The patch of red light may produce no marked reaction whatsoever (what reaction does appear will depend upon previous conditioning). But if I show the red light and then immediately or shortly thereafter stimulate my subject's hand with the electric current and repeat this routine often enough, the red light will cause the immediate withdrawal of the hand. The red light now becomes a substitute stimulus— it will call out the R whenever it stimulates the subject in that setting. Something has happened to bring about this change. This change, as we have pointed out, is called conditioning—the reaction remains the same but we have increased the number of stimuli that will call it out.[28]

The difference between Watson's classical conditioning approach and Thorndike's "law of effect" can be brought out by means of an example from Watson's book on child care.[29] Why is it that some children become very difficult to put to bed at night, and even seem terrified at the prospect? Classical conditioning focuses on the stimulus that originally called out the behavior and the substitute stimulus that might have become associated with it; so Watson postulated that the original fear response could have been produced by an angry parent forcing the child into bed, turning out the light, and then noisily slamming the door. Here the unconditioned or unlearned stimulus is the noise, which naturally produces a fear response, but a new conditioned stimulus becomes associated with the fear response, that is, going to bed and having the light turned out. The process can be represented diagramatically, as shown in Figure 2. On the

S ————————————————————————————————————▶ R
(Unconditioned)   Fear
Noise of slamming door
    or
(Conditioned)
Going to bed and light turned off

Figure 2

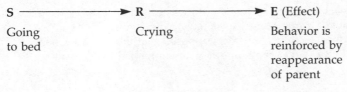

Figure 3

other hand, Thorndike's law of effect puts the emphasis, not on the *stimulus* evoking the behavior or reaction, but on the *effects* of the behavior. If the fear response has a desirable consequence, for instance, if mother comes and sits with the child or a light is left burning in the nursery, then the behavior is more likely to recur. This process is represented diagramatically in Figure 3.

Watson, blind to the significance of Thorndike's work, saw the mechanism of classical conditioning at work everywhere, and he warned parents of the "sledge-hammers" they were unknowingly using to shape their children's behavior.[30] He summed up:

> It is impossible to do more than just sketch in a few general words the way the human body becomes conditioned. The main point to emphasize is that practically every responding organ of the body can be conditioned; and that this conditioning takes place not only throughout adult life but can and does take place daily from the moment of birth (in all probability before birth). Most of this organization takes place below the verbalized level. . . . All of us are shot through with stimulus substitutions of one kind or another which we know nothing about until the behaviorist tries us out and tells us about them.[31]

§   §   §

THE behaviorist model of the child was developed to a new stage of sophistication by B. F. Skinner. Skinner had not originally intended to become a psychologist. He had taken college courses in English together with biological science in the hope of a career as an author, until he found that he had nothing of importance to say! In this uncertain state, Skinner came across articles written by Bertrand Russell that were philosophical critiques of Watson's work. In Skinner's words:

Many years later when I told Lord Russell that his articles were responsible for my interest in behavior, he could only exclaim, "Good Heavens! I have always supposed that those articles had demolished Behaviorism!" But at any rate he had taken Watson seriously, and so did I.[32]

Skinner enrolled for his Ph.D. in psychology, graduating from Harvard in 1931. The articles that had initially stimulated Skinner were incorporated by Russell into his book *An Outline of Philosophy* (1927).[33] In this book, which was contemporaneous with Watson's work and came out a year before the book on child care, Russell achieved a surprising perspective and foreshadowed something of the direction that Skinner's own work was to take. Russell appreciated, as Watson did not, that Thorndike's work was an essential complement to the behaviorist's attempt to account for behavior in terms of classical Pavlovian conditioning. He recognized, too, the link between Watson and the Lockean associationist tradition and, in general, expressed sympathy with much that Watson was attempting in psychology. Russell agreed that in order to progress psychology must use the methods of the physical sciences. His argument with Watson was that, in fact, the physical sciences were based upon a form of introspection. (In Russell's view, scientific knowledge was constructed out of the subjective sense experience of individuals.) Russell's argument, however, failed to convince the young Skinner.

Skinner persisted with his animals, and over the years he made numerous significant discoveries. He was responsible for advances in the technology of psychology, and for perfecting the "Skinner box," which delivered a reinforcing pellet of food to the animal inhabitant either at some fixed rate or when the animal had performed a set task such as pecking a lighted screen or pushing a lever. He also investigated various "schedules of reinforcement," such as giving the reinforcing morsel at regular or irregular time intervals, or after every successful performance of some predetermined task, or after some determined or irregular number of successful performances. And he invented the teaching machine, which reinforced the human student upon mastery of an item of knowledge—by the reward of the machine's acknowledgment of the correct response.

Another of his inventions was the "air crib," an enclosed box with a glass front and a movable roll of sheeting as a type of carpet. The box's air intake was filtered and could be warmed and humidified to a regulated level. Thus the box provided a controlled environment, the purpose of which Skinner revealed in the *Ladies Home Journal* in 1945:

> In that brave new world which science is preparing for the house-wife of the future, the young mother has apparently been for-gotten. Almost nothing has been done to ease her lot by simplifying and improving the care of babies. When we decided to have another child, my wife and I felt that it was time to apply a little labor-saving invention and design to the problems of the nursery. . . . We asked only one question: Is this practice impor-tant for the physical and psychological health of the baby?[34]

Skinner's daughter Deborah lived in the box, unencumbered by awk-ward and inefficient clothing, for several years. In the warm and germ-free atmosphere of the box she thrived, but of course she was taken out regularly for the usual cuddling and playing. Skinner found that the baby was particularly susceptible to small changes in temperature, a fact that had been masked from previous observers by the ineffi-ciency of layers of clothing to achieve an optimum temperature. In particular, he found that "crying and fussing could always be stopped by slightly lowering the temperature."[35]

The "air crib," however, was not central to Skinner's extension of the behaviorist model of the child. More relevant was his devel-opment of "operant conditioning," which was a continuation of Thorndike's work, except that Skinner avoided subjective expressions such as "satisfaction," which his predecessor had used when stating the law of effect. Almost as if he was following Bertrand Russell, Skinner frankly admitted the limitations of classical conditioning:

> Although the process of conditioning greatly extends the scope of the eliciting stimulus, it does not bring all the behavior of the organism within such stimulus control. According to the formula of stimulus substitution we must elicit a response before we can condition it. All conditioned reflexes are, therefore, based upon unconditioned reflexes. But we have seen that reflex responses are only a small part of the total behavior of the organism.[36]

Skinner then discussed Thorndike's work and introduced his own terminology. Whereas Thorndike had rewarded a response to "stamp" it in, Skinner focused on the responses that operated upon the orga-nism's environment, naming them "operants." "In operant condi-tioning we 'strengthen' an operant in the sense of making a response more probable or, in actual fact, more frequent."[37]

Skinner was able to "shape" the operant behavior of his research animals to a considerable extent, and he showed that if some complex operant was to be conditioned, it was not necessary to wait for its highly unlikely first occurrence before starting to reinforce the animals. He described his experience of teaching a pigeon to bowl. The plan was for the bird to swipe a ball with its head in such a way as to make the ball roll and knock miniature pins over. Skinner waited, ready to reward the first correct swipe:

> But nothing happened. Though we had all the time in the world, we grew tired of waiting. We decided to reinforce any response which had the slightest resemblance to a swipe—perhaps, at first, merely the behavior of looking at the ball—and then to select responses which more closely approximated the final form. The result amazed us. In a few minutes, the ball was caroming off the wall of the box as if the pigeon had been a champion squash player.[38]

Using this technique Skinner taught pigeons to steer guided missiles by pecking at the image of a target projected on a screen in the nose of the rocket as it homed in. He was also able to train dogs, rats, pigeons, and babies to do a variety of tasks.

Just as Watson saw classical conditioning everywhere, Skinner was preoccupied with operant conditioning; and this process became a key to his view of the child and the possibilities of perfecting the human species:

> While we are awake, we act upon the environment constantly, and many of the consequences of our actions are reinforcing. Through operant conditioning the environment builds the basic repertoire with which we keep our balance, walk, play games, handle instruments and tools, talk, write, sail a boat, drive a car, or fly a plane. . . . operant reinforcement does more than build a behavioral repertoire. It improves the efficiency of behavior and maintains behavior in strength long after acquisition or efficiency has ceased to be of interest.[39]

Skinner pushed the behaviorists' environmentalistic and deterministic thesis to its logical conclusion. The behavior of mankind needed reforming if wars, pollution, and overpopulation were to be avoided, and if the development of literature and the arts was to be encouraged, but, nevertheless, it had to be recognized that the world had become what it was by the contingencies of reinforcement provided by the environment. Hence, to reform human behavior the environment had to be reformed; it had to be so arranged that socially desirable behavior was reinforced, rather than the random host of often disruptive or potentially disruptive types of behavior that were conditioned at present.

Skinner did not shy away from the fact that the view he was canvassing destroyed the image of a person as a free or autonomous being. He claimed this was a remnant of a prescientific way of thinking:

> By questioning the control exercised by autonomous man and demonstrating the control exercised by the environment, a science of behavior also seems to question dignity or worth. A person is responsible for his behavior, not only in the sense that he may be justly blamed or punished when he behaves badly, but also in the sense that he is to be given credit and admired for his achievements. A scientific analysis shifts the credit as well as the blame to the environment.[40]

A completely controlled environment was, of course, out of reach at present. Here Skinner's literary interests were relevant, and he dramatized his ideas in the novel *Walden Two* (1948), which depicted a commune established in a rural part of the United States by Frazier, a brilliant behavioral scientist. From birth onward the inhabitants lived in an environment that was designed to reinforce socially desirable behavior. Young children lived in an environment that was directly controlled by adults, such as the air crib, but as they grew the direct controls were gradually replaced by indirect and social factors. In one passage Frazier explained to his visitors how members of the community refused to reinforce anyone's boring behavior; instead of politely feigning attention, and so making it more likely that the behavior would be repeated, they yawned or just walked off. (It is interesting to compare Skinner's vision of communal living with Bruno Bettelheim's study of child rearing in the kibbutzim of Israel in his *Children of the Dream*.[41])

In the course of the novel Skinner responded to some of the obvious criticisms. The answer to the question of who actually determined what behavior was socially desirable was that it was not a question of one person or even a small group imposing a solution, rather, it was a matter for experimentation and for consensus within the community. Again the issue of determinism versus freedom was squarely faced; in one incident Frazier confronted his critic, Castle, with the question "What would you do if you found yourself in possession of an effective science of behavior? Suppose you suddenly found it possible to control the behavior of men as you wished?" It was part of Frazier's case that the Nazis, the clinical psychologist, the educator, the politician, the advertising agent, and the priest all knew something about the shaping of behavior:

> "What would I do?" said Castle thoughtfully. "I think I would dump your science of behavior in the ocean."
> "And deny men all the help you could otherwise give them?"
> "And give them the freedom they would otherwise lose forever!"
> "How could you give them freedom?"
> "By refusing to control them!"
> "But you would only be leaving the control in other hands."
> "Whose?"
> "The charlatan, the demagogue, the salesman, the ward healer, the bully, the cheat, the educator, the priest—all who are in possession of the techniques of behavioral engineering."[42]

And a little later in the conversation, when tackled again on the question of freedom, Frazier replied: "I deny that freedom exists at all. I must deny it—or my program would be absurd."[43]

§ § §

OPPONENTS of determinism have had a hard road to travel. It is not only that the arguments of Watson and Skinner were put forward in an extremely clear and engaging way—their points also had a great deal of rational force. It is surely a commonplace belief that all events that occur in the world do so because of prior causes, and that those causes are themselves the result of (that is, are caused by) even earlier events. Insofar as human actions are events that occur in the world, it would seem to follow that human actions are caused by prior events— and thus we are ensnared by determinism. Of course, there is no escape in claiming that most of the time individuals do not *feel* fully determined by prior causes; the determinist will argue, as Watson would have argued against Huxley's Savage, that this feeling is merely an illusion. For if some action is performed, or not performed, some prior event caused that act or non-act. And given that the prior causal event did occur, the later act seemingly had to occur, despite the agent's belief about how much freedom there was to choose how to act in that situation.

The final plank in the determinist's platform seems decisive: it is argued that the alternative view—"indeterminism"—is indefensible, for would a person want to claim that any of his or her actions were uncaused? If, for example, an individual were to stand up and leave the room, would anyone want to claim this was uncaused? The agent might not know why he or she left the room—perhaps on an impulse—but even the agent would hold that *something* caused the action. A related issue is that if some human actions are uncaused, then the individuals involved could not be held morally responsible for them, a consequence that could have a fatal impact on our legal system.

The determinists have not had it all their own way, however. In a recent book, *The Nature of the Child*, Jerome Kagan acknowledges the various causal factors at work shaping the growing child—the biological forces, the influence of the family, and a range of social influences. But Kagan insists that how the child responds to these, and how the child balances these several forces, is not fully determined beforehand. Adults are not "continuous" with the children from whom they developed—an issue on which Kagan clearly differs from most previous writers, including Locke, Freud, and even Piaget. How an individual acts in any situation depends upon how he or she thinks about it, and humans have the capacity to come up with novel conceptualizations.

> Of course, past experience can make a significant contribution to the present. But if, in addition, one acknowledges the role of maturation of cognitive functions, temperamental qualities, and the possibility of discontinuity, one will attain a deeper understanding.[44]

A similar point has been made by the humanistic psychologist Carl Rogers. At a symposium where he debated the issue with Skinner, Rogers stated that

> one important way of knowing is through the formation of inner hypotheses, which are checked by referring to our inward flow of experiencing as we live in our subjective interaction with inner or outer events. This type of knowing is fundamental to everyday living.[45]

Rogers acknowledged that behaviorism has made many valuable contributions, but "time will indicate the unfortunate effects of the bounds it has tended to impose."[46] One cannot do justice to human psychology by ignoring the "inner meanings" and "purposes" that influence how people act.

Rogers also acknowledged that, in some respects, the behavioristic view that "man is a machine, a complicated but nonetheless understandable machine," is sound. So, too, is the Freudian view that "man is an irrational being, irrevocably in the grip of that past," especially via the influence of the repository of past experience—"the unconscious."[47] But there is a third view that also contains a true perspective, and which needs to be added to the previous two:

> [Man] is a person in the process of creating himself, a person who creates meaning in life, a person who embodies a dimension of subjective freedom. . . . he is able to live dimensions of his life which are not fully or adequately contained in a description of his conditionings or of his unconscious.[48]

It appears that Kagan and Rogers have tried to escape from the dilemma of choosing between determinism and indeterminism by finding a third alternative, namely, the one philosophers have called the theory of agency.[49] But Skinner, for one, was not convinced; the real causes of human behavior are the things the behaviorist studies: "I am *not* convinced that the things Dr. Rogers sees and infers are the primary moving forces. They seem to me to be epiphenomenal in a philosophical sense."[50] And to muddy the waters even further— and to indicate how complex are the set of issues surrounding the "free will *versus* determinism" debate—it should be noted that in the discussion following his paper in the symposium with Skinner, Rogers acknowledged that in scientific research, "he accepts the world as a determined world." But he also restated his equally strong belief that this "is not the whole of the truth about life."[51]

9.

THE THINKING MACHINE

It is evident that models of the child do not arise in a vacuum. The thought of Locke and Cotton Mather, of Rousseau and Neill, of Stanley Hall and Piaget, of Freud, of Dewey and Marx, and of Skinner and Rogers was in each case embedded in a complex intellectual and social environment. The models these men produced were shaped to an important degree by the philosophical, scientific, and religious ideas that were currently "in the air." The same is no doubt true of the ideas about children being forged in our own times.

It is interesting—and sobering—to speculate how people in later ages will characterize the twentieth century and what they will identify as the leading influence upon our thought. One candidate undoubtedly will be technology, for the history of the twentieth century has been riddled with achievements in this dimension: radio, TV, the automobile, the airplane, the spaceship, wonder drugs, birth control, organ transplants, genetic engineering, weapons of mass destruction. And, of course, the electronic computer.

The computer has not only revolutionized how research is conducted in the various disciplines, it is also rapidly becoming a source of analogies and heuristic ideas that are bearing fruit in a number of areas. It was inevitable that human cognition would be inspected from this perspective; for many researchers, computer science concepts are helpful analogies to be used in studying the human ability to reason, while for others there is no mere analogy—the brain is not like a computer, it *is* a computer. A new model of the child embodying this latter insight is in the process of emerging.

§   §   §

THERE is a well-known program, ELIZA, available for many personal computers, that mimics the behavior of an analyst. The computer will engage you in dialogue, asking you to discuss any psychological problems, and pressing for information about parents, siblings, and loved ones. The program's inventor, Joseph Weizenbaum, evidently had it in mind to show how easy it was to make a computer seem like a real person. He certainly succeeded; there is a story that on one occasion he came to his office to find a secretary engaged in a discussion with ELIZA, and he was asked to leave the room as the counseling session was private! And to take another example, the program PERDIX, devised by educational researchers at the University of Pittsburgh, can work through geometry problems in the style of a human learner, even making the same kind of mistakes as a novice. These, and other impressive achievements, illustrate that a computer can act like a human. But is a human in any way like a computer?

The view that a human is a type of machine, albeit a very special one that can think, is not of course a new product of the twentieth century. But there is now available a set of ideas to make the viewpoint more or less credible. Speculators in earlier ages drew for inspiration upon the technologies available in their own times, but those technologies were not able to throw convincing light on the human mind, no matter how ingenious were the arguments put forward to make the link. Even Freud, at the beginning of this century, could not get beyond a fairly crude level with his mechanistic idea of mental energy that behaved analogously to physical energy as depicted by Helmholtz.

Descartes, working in the first half of the seventeenth century, was familiar with the incredible clockwork mechanisms of his day, and with the mechanized statues that could move limbs realistically, which adorned the gardens of the aristocracy. He came to regard animals also as automata, differing little from the moving statues. Moreover, many of these statues were worked hydraulically, and Descartes thought the same was true of animals and of people. He tried to show "what must be the fabric of the nerves and muscles of the human body in order that the animal spirits therein contained should have the power to move the members."[1] Descartes went on:

> From this aspect the body is regarded as a machine which, having been made by the hands of God, is incomparably better arranged, and possesses in itself movements which are much more admirable, than any of those which can be invented by man.[2]

Descartes even recognized that a machine could, in principle, be constructed that would be able to utter words; for instance, a machine that might respond to being touched by asking what we wanted to say to it. "But," he said, "it never happens that it arranges its speech . . . in order to reply appropriately to everything that may be said in its presence, as even the lowest type of man can do." The identical issue was raised in a provocative and influential way about two hundred years later by Alan Turing, as we will see.

The great comparative anatomist of the second half of the nineteenth century (and the fluent defender and popularizer of Darwinism), T. H. Huxley, argued that if Descartes had been familiar with the advances in physiology that had been made in the intervening century, he would have been strongly confirmed in his opinions. Huxley, however, wanted to disagree, for he believed that although animals were automata, they were *conscious* automata:

> But though we may see reason to disagree with Descartes' hypothesis that brutes are unconscious machines, it does not follow that he was wrong in regarding them as automata. They may be more or less conscious, sensitive, automata.[3]

Huxley speculated that although humans think, their mental activity is merely the reflection of "molecular changes of the brain-substance." Thinking is not causally efficacious, and so we, along with the brutes, are conscious machines.

Another famous figure to hold a similar view was the materialist physician Julian Offray de La Mettrie. A contemporary of Descartes, he went much further and argued that the human soul was also mechanically produced. It was not contradictory to hold that a machine was able "to feel, to think, to know how to distinguish good from bad."

> I believe that thought is so little incompatible with organized matter, that it seems to be one of its properties on a par with electricity, the faculty of motion, impenetrability, extension, etc.[4]

This, however, is as far as these writers went toward explaining how the miracle of thought occurred. It was not until the development of the theory of the "Turing machine" that the path was clear for further development.

§   §   §

IN 1936, A. M. Turing published a paper "On Computable Numbers," in which he gave an account of a theoretical device—a logic

"machine"—that came to be called a "Turing machine." The point of
the paper was not to provide a blueprint for building a real machine,
but to throw theoretical light on problems in mathematics and logic
(for instance, whether certain problems can be solved by the repeated
application of a simple rule—the sort of procedure that a machine
can carry out). But the theoretical device that Turing described has
become, indeed, the logical heart of modern electronic computers.
J. David Bolter, in *Turing's Man*, points out that

> what Turing provided was a symbolic description, revealing only
> the logical structure and saying nothing about the realization of
> that structure (in relays, vacuum tubes, or transistors) . . . but
> no computer built in the intervening half century has surpassed
> these specifications.[5]

It is irrelevant, for the theory, of what a Turing machine is physically
composed; as Bolter said, it could be tubes or transistors, but it could
also be made of gears and cards (as in the physical machine designed
by the early nineteenth-century Cambridge mathematician Charles
Babbage). It could also conceivably be made of protoplasm, DNA,
and so on.

In 1950 Turing published, in the famous philosophy journal
Mind, a paper that was much less technical—"Computing Machinery
and Intelligence"[6]—which immediately stimulated widespread discussion. Setting out to consider the question "Can machines think?"
Turing quickly focused on another which he thought to be more
revealing. He outlined a game, in which an interrogator in one room
indirectly questioned (by typing out various queries) two individuals
in another room. The interrogator's task was to determine from the
answers, with 70 percent accuracy, whether both individuals were
human or whether one was a computer. Turing's query was whether
or not it was feasible for a computer (not necessarily one that exists
at present, but one that might exist before the end of the twentieth
century) to be indistinguishable from a human in five minutes of
questioning. (This, it will be recalled, is what Descartes claimed no
machine could possibly be.) It might be thought that Turing's game
poses an easy task; the questioner just has to ask each individual if
it is a computer. But while the human would say "no," a properly
programmed computer would also respond "no," for the point would
be for it to act as much like a human as possible.

Turing admitted that he could not prove that a humanlike computer could be built, but he strongly believed that it was feasible and

attempted to strengthen his case by answering the various arguments that he felt might be raised to show that such a thing was not possible in principle. He also discussed some of the theoretical issues in the design of such a device. He stated his conviction that "at the end of the century the use of words and general educated opinion will have altered so much that one will be able to speak of machines thinking without expecting to be contradicted."[7]

Toward the end of his paper, Turing reflected upon the best way to proceed if the challenge of building such a computer within fifty years was to be met successfully. The engineering problems were likely, he felt, to be no great stumbling block—it looked, in 1950, as if the requisite speed, memory storage, and so on, could all be easily obtained. (And, of course, he was right.) But he was concerned that programming in all the specific items of information, and all the skills, needed to simulate an adult human being was likely to be a slow and difficult task. Turing hit upon an interesting strategy:

> Instead of trying to produce a program to simulate the adult mind, why not try to produce one that simulates the child's? If this were then subjected to an appropriate course of education one would obtain the adult brain. Presumably the child-brain is something like a notebook as one buys it from the stationers. Rather little mechanism, and lots of blank sheets. . . . We have thus divided our problem into two parts—The child-program and the education process.[8]

He was realistic in his expectations—the first attempts to find the right child-machine might not be successful, and "it will not be possible to apply exactly the same teaching process to the machine as to a normal child."

It can be argued that Turing's test was successfully met about twenty years earlier than he had imagined it would. ELIZA is very lifelike, and PERDIX behaves very much like an adolescent student of geometry. The strategy of constructing a computer that can learn from "experience" is still being actively pursued. Whether we would grant that such machines and programs are capable of "thought" is more of a moot point; as one of Turing's early critics pointed out, a machine that closely mimics a human *appears* very human, and for some purposes it might be better to use the machine rather than a person, but this doesn't mean that the machine is *the same* as a person.[9]

After 1950 there was a flurry of activity. By 1958, Herbert Simon (who was later to win the Nobel prize) predicted—rashly, as it turned out—that within ten years a computer program would be the chess champion of the world; and two years later G. Miller, E. Galanter, and K. Pribram published an influential book exploring the computer as an analogy for human mentality.[10]

But this is not the end of the story; Turing's work has helped to stimulate work in another direction—the notion of treating a computer like a child needing education can be stood on its head. The child can be thought of as a sophisticated Turing machine, and the child's growth to maturity can be looked at in programming terms. As the authors of one textbook have written:

> The impact of computer science on cognitive psychology, then, has been profound on several dimensions. First, it supplied us with a new set of ideas on symbolic processes, a new methodology, and a new way of expressing our theories: computer simulation. . . . It supplied concepts by which theories of internal events could be developed—for example, storage, retrieval, buffer device, executive control, and the notation of graph networks. It gave us a new perspective on the human organism, in which man is viewed as a general-purpose symbol manipulator of fascinating complexity and considerable efficiency.[11]

In a word, the computer has become the source of a new model or paradigm, one that is still developing.

§   §   §

A TYPICAL personal computer consists of some input device—a console or keyboard; it has some inbuilt processing capabilities, including perhaps some permanent "intelligence" or "knowledge" (it is difficult to avoid anthropomorphic language)—so many "k" of ROM, for instance; it has a working memory or RAM— recently 64k was common, but now 256k is not unusual; and it has permanent memory into and out of which information is transferred—these days floppy disks can store hundreds of pages of information, and hard disks with enormous storage capacity are becoming popular. The computer has an inbuilt language by which it operates, and the information is manipulated and transferred in one or another standard form, such as ASCII. Finally, it has several alternative output devices, such as a screen or printer, or a modem by which it communicates with other computers.

According to the new paradigm, a person can be thought of as being structured in a parallel way, and research aimed at elucidating this has been very fruitful. Consider a young child—perhaps Piaget's one-year-old Lucienne, who was introduced in Chapter 6. The child receives data through the sense organs; the child also has some inborn processing capacities—otherwise it would not be able to learn—but in addition, some "information" or "programs" are built-in at birth (for example, the child does not have to learn how to suck, for this is an innate reflex); there is a working memory, in which the child keeps those items of knowledge and skill that are being used at a particular moment; and there is a permanent memory, which is, in Locke's terms, largely a "blank tablet" at birth, but which has a storage capacity that makes a hard disk pale into insignificance. The child gradually builds up a symbolic representation of the world around it, so there must be some inner "language" or medium of representation; even a newborn baby is starting to see and taste and smell and hear and touch, and to remember the more striking of its experiences, so the internal medium by which it represents and stores these impressions cannot be the native language (of which it is still ignorant). Jerry Fodor has discussed this inbuilt "language of thought," which is similar conceptually to the "machine language" that is built into the personal computer and about which most users remain completely ignorant.[12] (The user of a computer may be entering commands in English, but the computer does not process or store the items as English words.)

There may be one or two important exceptions to the generalization that permanent memory is empty at birth. If the Freudians and others are right, or even on the right track, there may be inborn memory traces of the racial past. And if Noam Chomsky is right, there may be a genetically determined innate framework that serves as the basis for the child's acquisition of its native language; in other words, the child may not have to build up for itself, completely from scratch, its understanding of the native language, for the "skeleton," at least, may be inborn. Children in different cultures will flesh out this skeleton in different ways—one will plug in data about English and will come to speak this language, while another may pad the skeleton with data about Spanish. As Chomsky put it,

> It is the mechanism of language acquisition that is innate. In a given linguistic community, children with very different experience arrive at comparable grammars, indeed almost identical ones, so far as we know. That is what requires explanation. Even within a very narrow community —take the elite in Paris—the experiences are varied. Each child has a different experience, each child

is confronted by different data—but in the end the system is essentially the same. As a consequence we have to suppose that all children share the same internal constraints which characterize narrowly the grammar they are going to construct.[13]

There are many other unresolved issues. The size, and development, of working memory has been one concern; it was suggested earlier that Piaget did not consider developmental deficiencies here as a possible cause of Lucienne's not being able to find a hidden object. But there is a well-known finding that an adult can accommodate about seven bits of information, plus or minus two, in working memory at any one time. (The term "bit" is somewhat misleading, for a bit can be quite complex, providing that its parts are closely interrelated.) It has also been determined that it takes on the order of four or five seconds to transfer a "chunk" of information from working memory into permanent storage. Furthermore, much information is never transferred and is lost forever. Thus, adults have trouble remembering a new telephone number that they have just looked up in the directory, and they spontaneously adopt the strategy of "rehearsing" or repeating it until they have dialed (a strategy that keeps the information in working memory until the job is done). The infant is less sophisticated, with consequent lapses in performance.

When solving a problem, the adult has to transfer the relevant information from long-term or permanent storage into working memory, a task that has two aspects: a judgment of relevance has to be made, and the requisite knowledge has to be located in the "memory banks." Here there has been a great deal of research. Do humans search for information serially or in parallel—in other words, can more than one search proceed at the same time? How is information filed? Herbert Simon stated, in his Compton lectures, that

> we are led to the hypothesis that memory is an organization of list structures (lists whose components can also be lists), which include descriptive components (two-termed relations) and short (three-element or four-element) component lists.

And he added:

> The evidence is overwhelming that the system is basically serial in its operation: that it can process only a few symbols at a time and that the symbols being processed must be held in special, limited memory structures whose content can be changed rapidly.[14]

Furthermore, there is some evidence (although the matter is controversial) that there is an "executive" that selects which strategies and information will be brought to bear on a problem. The difference between "bright" and "dull" children seems to lie, according to this evidence, in the functioning of this selection mechanism rather than in the range of skills that children of different abilities actually possess (for often there is no great difference on this dimension). There has been some discussion of whether or not this view places a "ghost" or "homunculus" into the child's cognitive apparatus—intelligent children are intelligent because they have an intelligent executive, a theory that, on its face, replaces one mystery with another.[15]

A variety of research techniques have been used to investigate these matters. One already alluded to is computer modeling. A program such as PERDIX is written, based on clearly stated assumptions about how the computer will process the information that is fed into it; if the result is that the computer plus program acts in a way that closely resembles the way in which a human learner or problem solver behaves in the same situation, that at least is *some* indication that the researcher might be on to something. A careful analysis of errors that students make is also sometimes revealing. But perhaps the basic research technique involves reaction times.

Consider a hypothetical but nonetheless feasible experiment in what is known as the "fast-process" research tradition. A simple question is devised and then phrased in different ways, for example, negatively and positively. (Thus, "If John is taller than Bill, is Bill shorter than John?" and "If Bill is not as tall as John, is John not as short as Bill?") The question might also be so worded that the answer to one form of it is "yes," and to another form, "no." Different groups of students are then exposed to these alternate forms via a computer console. The time taken for answers to be selected —how long it takes for the "yes" or "no" button to be pushed—is measured in microseconds. The results, typically, are that questions posed negatively take longer to solve, and that correct statements can be recognized more rapidly than incorrect ones. From this sort of data, inferences can be drawn about the complexity of the corresponding mental operations, the processes by which students judge the identity of statements couched in alternative forms, and so forth. Robert Sternberg has given a clear account of the logic of the "additive" and "subtractive" methods used here, the general idea being that if a complex mental process is made up of parts (say a + b), and if the time taken for the whole process can be measured, then the time taken for each part can be determined by devising a related task that has one less or one more part. (Thus, if a task involving only "a" was devised, then "b" could be determined by subtraction from "a + b," or if a task involving "a + b + c" could be timed, then the time for "c" could be deduced.)[16]

This general "information processing" or "cognitive science" approach to child development has started to bear fruit in education. When one is working with a piece of processing equipment, whether it be a computer or a student, it is only common sense to bear in mind the limitations that it possesses. There is growing awareness among curriculum experts that every item of knowledge and skill that the learner requires to master a domain must be accounted for. And the student must not be given just information, but must also be guided as to how to structure or relate the items that have been presented, for the child will be building memory structures. Piaget and Dewey were right in depicting the child as an active inquirer—learning is not a passive absorption process (more or less as depicted by Locke). Donald Norman, one of the key workers in the new paradigm, has put it powerfully:

> What goes on in the mind of the learner? A lot: People who are learning are active, probing, constructing. People appear to have a strong desire to understand. The problem is that people will go to great lengths to understand, constructing frameworks, constructing explanations, constructing huge edifices to account for what they have experienced. . . . But, like a theorist, a learner builds on incomplete evidence, tends to ignore evidence that does not fit, and will grasp at any evidence that can serve as confirmation. It is often surprising what learners come to believe.[17]

This, then, is "Turing's man." According to this emerging model, in the long run a human may not be distinguishable from a data-processing machine in a Turing test because a human *is* a data-processing machine. Only time will tell whether the model will become dominant and endure, or whether—like most others—it will have its time in the sun and then fade away, leaving, though, some legacy for the future. But even at this stage of the model's development it is clear that it has stimulated a major change in the way we talk about thinking and learning—"computerese" is an accepted idiom, even among those who do not possess a silicon chip or a floppy disk.

10.

POSTSCRIPT

OVER the years, a variety of conceptions or paradigms of childhood have influenced the way humans have understood, cared for, and educated their young. Basically, the present book has put forward a two-way analysis of this phenomenon. On the one hand, it has focused on major ideas and themes from the relevant traditions in Western thought. On the other, it has concentrated on leading individuals and demonstrated how theoretical constructs worked in shaping their thought. The discussion has tried to indicate how even the most original models owed much to what went before them; indeed, to understand something of the history is to be on the way to understanding the strengths and weaknesses of each model.

All of us have our own sets of concepts and beliefs that influence how we perceive and interact with the surrounding world. In constructing these individual frameworks, each of us has absorbed much from the great paradigms or models that form the cultural heritage of our society, though we may not be aware of all this and may not have ensured that the pieces we have absorbed are theoretically compatible. One of the aims of our book has been to sensitize the reader to the vital role played by these major theories in our daily lives—theory-laden perception is a fact of life, and a fact we are well advised not to ignore.

Finally, we have aimed throughout to give the impression that history is not finished. Western thought is still dynamic; old models are capable of sudden rebirth, and it is possible for new models to arise. Perhaps among our readers there is someone who might be creating a new framework, a paradigm that will give fresh insight and that may supplant some older model; even so, the model will not have sprung forth completely *ex nihilo*—it will inevitably owe something to the very models it has supplanted.

§   §   §

A POSTSCRIPT permits the raising of issues complementary to a volume's major purpose. A number of matters cropped up in the preceding discussions but were not pursued because they would have distracted attention from the main themes then being developed. Several of them deserve further discussion in these closing pages: they pertain to the construction, operation, and assessment of models or paradigms of the child.

In the first place, a reader may in all fairness ask, "How can we decide between models? That is, on what grounds should we prefer one paradigm rather than another?" The obvious answer—that we should prefer a paradigm that is *true*—is not of much help in practice. The issue then becomes the equally intractable one of "How is the truth of such diverse models, with such diverse assumptions and underpinnings, determinable?" Probably the best that can be done is to say that a number of criteria should be borne in mind when studying models: their internal coherence, whether or not their metaphysical assumptions are reasonable in the light of the best knowledge we have at present, their fruitfulness in highlighting interesting and important phenomena that might otherwise be overlooked, and whether or not some of the consequences that can be derived from the model have successfully survived strong empirical testing (if, indeed, empirical testing is pertinent to the model).

Some of the urgency of having to choose between models is alleviated by the fact that many of them are "orthogonal" to each other; that is, strictly speaking, they are not incompatible for they focus on different aspects of the nature of the child. The theories of Freud and Piaget can probably coexist; so can those of Marx and Piaget, or Skinner and Marx, or Norman and Dewey.

It is important to bear in mind that there is something to be learned, too, even from a model that is clearly wrong. There are few today who would say that cognitive development proceeds in the atomistic manner depicted by Locke, but it would be boorish to say that there was nothing to be learned by studying his ideas, which were a major influence on more than two centuries of Western thought. Walter Goldschmidt, writing in the foreword to the popular *The Teachings of Don Juan*, pointed out that the central importance of entering into worlds other than our own . . . lies in the fact that the experience leads us to understand that our own world is also a cultural construct. By experiencing other worlds, then, we see our own for what it is.[1]

What is being advocated here is a degree of tolerance or charity and intellectual adventuresomeness with respect to rival models. There is, however, a danger associated with being too eclectic. One cannot build a "superordinate" model composed of random delicacies selected willy-nilly, for the end product might be intellectually incoherent. Environmentalistic ingredients do not mix well with hereditarian, and deterministic ones go poorly with indeterministic. If it is believed that human action is influenced by the activities of mind, then radical behaviorism would seem to be inadmissible.

Inconsistency when moving from one framework to another is one matter. But what of inconsistency within a paradigm—is it really a drawback? And is it a deficiency if a framework is not capable of empirical testing (that is, if it is metaphysical)? The issues here are complex, but it is clear that an inconsistent theory cannot be true, considered as a totality. For instance, there is something wrong with a framework that says that mind both exists and does not exist, although of course there is nothing inconsistent in saying that mind exists but is unimportant for understanding human behavior (a position that a charitable interpretation will attribute to the radical behaviorists). The source of the inconsistency would be important to ferret out—the framework may still be in the process of development, and a young position probably should be treated generously to allow time for it to mature.

The fact that a paradigm is metaphysical is no great drawback; metaphysical theses, such as the existence of mind or the innate goodness of humans or the nature of individuals as self-causing agents, are important and exert great influence upon those who accept them— as our discussions of Freud, Rousseau, Neill, and Rogers should have illustrated. And Popper, a hard-nosed intellect if ever there was one, reminds us that although metaphysical doctrines are not subject to definitive empirical testing, they are discussable and criticizable:

These theories describe some facts, but in the manner of myths. They contain most interesting psychological suggestions, but not in a testable form. At the same time I realized that such myths may be developed, and become testable; that historically speaking all—or very nearly all—scientific theories originate from myths. . . .

I thus felt that if a theory is found to be non-scientific, or "meta-physical" (as we might say), it is not thereby found to be unimportant, or insignificant, or "meaningless," or "nonsensical."[2]

It should also be clear that not everyone who accepts the same framework will see its implications in identical ways. A fine example of this is provided by the history of the impact of Lockeanism. Like all good models, even simple ones, Locke's meant different things to different people. As indicated in Chapter 2, some were impressed most by the origin of ideas in experience and developed this in various ways (Pestalozzi and Montessori); others focused upon the innate faculties or powers and explored these (the faculty psychologists and the phrenologists); while another group investigated the ways in which ideas were combined (the associationists). The same phenomenon can be found among the followers of Freud, Dewey, and the others discussed in the previous chapters of this book. And although many of them may have been following unproductive trails, nothing was lost and much was gained by posterity.

Finally, it is clear that the concepts developed by adherents of these various paradigms provide a legacy that is available to help in dealing with the experiences open to us today. Donald Schon has investigated the processes by which concepts grow and are replaced, and has concluded:

> New concepts are neither illusions nor law-like recombinations of old ones. New concepts do not spring from nothingness or from mysterious external sources. They come from old ones. . . . new concepts emerge out of the interaction of old concepts and new situations, where the old concept is not simply re-applied unchanged to a new instance but is that *in terms* of which the new instance is seen. This is . . . a process in which old concepts, in order to function as projective models for new situations, come themselves to be seen in new ways.[3]

§   §   §

METHODOLOGICAL questions aside, it is useful to look beyond the social and natural sciences when considering ways that models can influence our perceptions of children. Paradigms are communicated by other channels, including the arts. Although it is not possible to detail here the changing views transmitted through the medium of literature and the expressive arts, these sources of influence deserve pointing to in any discussion of the broader setting. (Skinner was not the first to expound and propagate his views via a novel.) To look back in time, during the romantic revival authors such as William Blake and William Wordsworth reversed the lack of interest in the state of the child within the field of literature.[4] Some of this new concern was inspired by Rousseau and his disciples, who declared that children had their own feelings and concerns. If Philippe Aries is to be believed, although strictly speaking his writing was only about France, during this period there was growing awareness that childhood was a stage of life distinct from adulthood. Thus, the stage was set for childhood to emerge as a theme in nineteenth- and twentieth-century English and American literature, a development that was considerably enhanced by the writing of Freud on the psychological and emotional importance of the earliest years. The lively world of the writer's imagination began to feed and interact with newly minted perceptions from other fields. There is little need to remark on the interest in children and childhood displayed by writers like Henry James, Charles Dickens, and Mark Twain.

The complication here is that at the same time awareness was increasing, childhood also was becoming an artistic symbol. Thus, the depiction of a child in many branches of art might not always have been intended to be realistic, but rather symbolic of such things as innocence, purity, and helplessness. Little Nell and Tiny Tim were not Dickens's attempts at realistic portrayal of nineteenth-century British juveniles. Perhaps some historians of childhood have not been as aware of this point as they should when they have been interpreting paintings of families and children from earlier ages.

The paradigms at work in literature are also at work in the field of biography. If the theme of our book holds true, it could be expected that the work of biographers would be shaped by the dominant theories of childhood of their times.[5] Typically, great men and women are depicted as having model childhoods by the standards of the biographers' day, or, in the case of great villains, model-flawed childhoods. Furthermore, the childhood of the very same individual may be treated differently at different times; what was deemed a minor alienation or as not worthy of mention by a nineteenth-century biographer might be regarded as a major crisis point by a writer in the twentieth.[6] Indeed, it is possible to date many biographies within a fairly narrow time span by analyzing the descriptions that are presented of the childhood period.

Models of childhood, then, are disseminated in diverse ways— through the theories of philosophers and psychologists, through childcare handbooks, through the arts and the various popular media, through biographies, and by word of mouth, which remains as popular as ever. And it is not only parents, teachers, and educational researchers who fall heir to the latest perceptions—for children themselves hold sets of ideas about their own childhoods, as evidenced in distinctive youth cultures, movements for children's rights, the contents of diaries kept by schoolchildren, and, of course, the ideas that persist about their childhoods when they have grown to maturity.

§   §   §

JEROME KAGAN has recently given a nice capsule statement of the main thesis of our book:

> The behavior of the infant is so ambiguous it is easy for the culture's beliefs about human nature to influence observers' interpretations of what they think they see. These influences are nicely illustrated in the different descriptions of the infant by Sigmund Freud, Erik Erikson, and Jean Piaget. Each of these influential theorists highlighted a special aspect of the child's first year because of suppositions originating in the larger cultural context in which each scholar lived.[7]

But it is not only infants who are subject to being seen in theory-laden ways, and it was not only Freud, Erikson, and Piaget who were influenced by the theories they had absorbed and adapted. As Helvétius realized, "Man is a model exposed to the view of different artists; every one surveys it from some point of view, no one from every point."

NOTES

1. ON SEEING CHILDREN THROUGHOUT HISTORY

1. Norwood R. Hanson, *Patterns of Discovery* (Cambridge: Cambridge University Press, 1965), p. 22.
2. The classic philosophical discussion of this is in Ludwig Wittgenstein, *Philosophical Investigations* (Oxford: Blackwell, 1963), p. 212e.
3. See M. L. Johnson Abercrombie, *The Anatomy of Judgement* (Harmondsworth, Middlesex: Penguin, 1969), pt. 1; also Thomas S. Kuhn, *The Structure of Scientific Revolutions* (Chicago: University of Chicago Press, 1968), ch. 10.
4. Abercrombie, op. cit., p. 44.
5. Ibid., p. 47.
6. Richard L. Gregory, *The Intelligent Eye* (London: Weidenfeld & Nicholson, 1970).
7. See Peter Coveney, *The Image of Childhood* (Harmondsworth, Middlesex: Penguin, 1967).
8. Mary Hesse, *Models and Analogies in Science* (London: Sheed & Ward, 1963).
9. A. S. Neill, *Summerhill* (New York: Hart, 1964), p. 95.
10. Kuhn, op. cit., pp. 10–11.
11. For criticisms of Kuhn, see Imre Lakatos and Alan Musgrave, eds., *Criticism and the Growth of Knowledge* (Cambridge: Cambridge University Press, 1970).
12. See Denis C. Phillips, "On What Scientists Know," in Elliot Eisner, ed., *Learning and Teaching the Ways of Knowing*, 84th Yearbook of the National Society for the Study of Education (Chicago: University of Chicago Press, 1985).
13. Philippe Aries, *Centuries of Childhood* (London: Jonathan Cape, 1962), p. 128.
14. Ibid., p. 133.

15. Lloyd de Mause, "Our Forebears Made Childhood a Nightmare," *Psychology Today*, April 1975, p. 85.
16. Neil Postman, *The Disappearance of Childhood* (New York: Laurel, 1982), p. 120.
17. Dorothy Suransky, *The Erosion of Childhood* (Chicago: University of Chicago Press, 1982), p. 187.
18. John Sommerville, *The Rise and Fall of Childhood* (Beverley Hills, Calif.: Sage, 1982), p. 12.
19. William Boyd, *The History of Western Education* (London: A. & C. Black, 1964).
20. John L. Davies, *A Short History of Women* (London: Thinkers Library, 1938), p. 34.
21. Ibid., p. 33.
22. Plato, *Republic* (Harmondsworth, Middlesex: Penguin, 1956), tr. H. D. P. Lee, pp. 208–9.
23. Jean Jacques Rousseau, *Emile* (London: Dent, Everyman's Library, 1955), tr. Barbara Foxley, p. 328.
24. Views of Anne Koedt and Mary Ellman in Leslie Tanner, ed., *Voices From Women's Liberation* (New York: Signet, 1971).
25. Germaine Greer, *The Female Eunuch* (London: Paladin, 1970), p. 91.
26. Shulamith Firestone, *The Dialectic of Sex* (London: Paladin, 1971), pp. 48–50.

2. THE CHILD AND THE ENVIRONMENT

1. Hans J. Eysenck, "The Dangers of the New Zealots," *Encounter*, December 1972, p. 91.
2. Arthur R. Jensen, "How Much Can We Boost IQ and Scholastic Achievement?" *Harvard Educational Review* 39 (1969), p. 3.
3. Ibid., p. 84.
4. For a balanced treatment of Burt's work, and for details of the fraud, see Leslie S. Hearnshaw, *Cyril Burt: Psychologist* (Ithaca, N.Y.: Cornell University Press, 1979).
5. Ibid., p. 4.
6. Ibid.
7. James L. Axtell, *The Educational Writings of John Locke* (Cambridge: Cambridge University Press, 1968), pp. 98–103.
8. John Locke, *An Essay Concerning Human Understanding* (London: Dent, Everyman's Library, 1959), ed. Raymond Wilburn, bk. 1, ch. 2, p. 5.
9. Ibid., bk. 2, ch. 1, p. 26.
10. Ibid.
11. Ibid., bk. 2, ch. 2, p. 34.
12. Reprinted in Howard Penniman, ed., *On Politics and Education* (New York: Van Nostrand, 1947), p. 210, par. 1.

13. John Locke, *An Essay Concerning Human Understanding*, bk. 2, ch. 13, p. 75.
14. See ibid., bk. 2, ch. 12, pp. 64–5, and bk. 3.
15. Ibid., bk. 4, ch. 20, p. 347.
16. Etienne Bonnot de Condillac, "Dedication," in *Treatise on the Sensations* (London: Faril Press, 1930), tr. Geraldine Carr.
17. Ibid., p. 239.
18. Clause Adrien Helvétius, *A Treatise on Man; His Intellectual Faculties and His Education*, 2 vols. (New York: Burt Franklin Press, 1969; reprint of 1810 edition), tr. W. Hooper, vol. 1, p. iii.
19. Ibid., p. vii.
20. Ibid., p. 3.
21. Ibid, pp. 6–7.
22. See John Passmore, *The Perfectibility of Man*, 2 vols. (London: Duckworth, 1970), especially vol. 1, ch. 8, 9.
23. Helvétius, op. cit., p. 12 (section heading).
24. Ibid., vol. 2, p. 403.
25. F. J. Gladman, *School Work* (London: Jarrold, 1886), pp. 120–1.
26. Ibid.
27. *Lessons on Objects: As Given to Children Between the Ages of Six and Eight in a Pestalozzian School, at Cheam, Surrey*, 17th ed. (London: Seeley, Jackson & Halliday, 1861), pp. 5–7.
28. John Locke, *Of the Conduct of the Understanding* (New York: Merril, 1901), p. 30.
29. See, for example, Herbert Spencer's famous essay "What Knowledge Is of Most Worth?" in his *Essays on Education*.
30. John Henry Newman, *On the Scope and Nature of University Education* (London: Dent, Everyman's Library, 1956), pp. 152–3.
31. John D. Davies, *Phrenology: Fad and Science* (New Haven: Yale University Press, 1955), pt. 1.
32. Herbert Spencer, *An Autobiography* (London: Williams & Norgate, 1904), vol. 1, p. 201.
33. See Walter B. Kolesnik, *Mental Discipline in Modern Education* (Madison: University of Wisconsin Press, 1958).
34. Thomas D. Cook et al., *"Sesame Street" Revisited* (New York: Russell Sage Foundation, 1975), p. 30.
35. Hans J. Eysenck, *Race, Intelligence, and Education* (London: Sun Books, 1971), pp. 129–30.
36. Ibid., pp. 139–40.

3. THE FREE AND THE CONSTRAINED CHILD

1. Quoted in John A. Newton, *Susanna Wesley and the Puritan Tradition in Methodism* (London: Epworth Press, 1968), p. 108.
2. Robert Southey, *The Life of Wesley* (London: Oxford University Press, 1925), vol. 2, pp. 304–5.

3. Quoted in Phillip J. Greven, ed., *Child-Rearing Concepts, 1628–1861: Historical Sources* (Itasca, Ill.: F. E. Peacock, 1973), pp. 61–2.
4. Ibid., p. 66.
5. N. Curnock, ed., *The Journal of the Rev. John Wesley, A.M.* (London: Epworth Press, 1938; reprint of 1909 edition), vol. 3, p. 357.
6. Greven, op. cit., p. 44.
7. Ibid., p. 45.
8. Arthur P. Stanley, *The Life and Correspondence of Thomas Arnold, D.D.* (London: B. Fellowes, 1852), vol. 1, p. 145 et passim.
9. Ibid., p. 96.
10. Ray C. Stedman et al., *Family Life* (Waco, Tex.: Word Books, 1976), p. 83.
11. Ibid.
12. Garner T. Armstrong, *The Plain Truth About Child Rearing* (Pasadena, Calif.: Ambassador College Press, 1970).
13. Ibid., p. 46.
14. Greven, op. cit., p. 13.
15. Ibid., p. 48.
16. Ibid., p. 101.
17. Quoted in H. Mathews, *Methodism and the Education of the People, 1791–1851* (London: Epworth Press, 1949), p. 20.
18. Jean Jacques Rousseau, *Emile* (London: Dent, Everyman's Library, 1955), tr. Barbara Foxley, p. 5.
19. Ibid., p. 56.
20. Ibid.
21. Ibid., p. 55.
22. Ibid., p. 57.
23. Ibid., p. 84.
24. Ibid., p. 28.
25. Harriet Jessie and Harold Edgeworth Butler, *The Black Book of Edgeworthstown* (London: Faber & Gwyer, 1927), p. 137.
26. Ibid., p. 146.
27. Ibid., p. 140.
28. Ibid.
29. Quoted in William A. Stewart and William P. McCann, *The Educational Innovators* (London: Macmillan, 1967), pp. 33–4.
30. Curnock, op. cit., vol. 5, pp. 352–3.
31. See "Introduction" by A. S. Neill, in Homer Lane, *Talks to Parents and Teachers* (New York: Schocken, 1969).
32. A. S. Neill, *Summerhill* (New York: Hart, 1964), p. 250.
33. Ibid.
34. Ibid., p. 4.
35. Bertrand Russell, *On Education, Especially in Early Childhood* (London: George, Allen & Unwin, 1930), pp. 32–3.
36. Joe Park, *Bertrand Russell on Education* (London: Allen & Unwin, 1964), p. 114.

4. THE CHILD AND THE SPECIES

1. For a discussion of von Baer and his influence on Darwin, see Jane Oppenheimer, "An Embryological Enigma in the *Origin of Species*," in Bentley Glass, Owsei Temkin, and William Strauss, eds., *Forerunners of Darwin, 1745–1859* (Baltimore: Johns Hopkins Press, 1959).
2. See the reference to Kohlbrugge in Glass, Temkin, and Strauss, op. cit., p. 293.
3. Quoted in Glass, Temkin, and Strauss, op. cit., p. 301.
4. Ibid., pp. 292–313; also Erik Nordenskiold, *The History of Biology* (New York: Tudor, n.d.), pp. 363–6.
5. Charles Darwin, *On the Origin of Species* (New York: Mentor, 1959; reprint of 6th ed. of 1872), p. 416.
6. Ernst Haeckel, *The History of Creation*, vol. 1, ch. 13 (originally published in 1873); reprinted in Robert E. Grinder, *A History of Genetic Psychology* (New York: John Wiley & Sons, 1967), p. 112.
7. Benjamin Spock, *Baby and Child Care* (New York: Pocket Books, 1963; 127th printing of the new ed. of *The Pocket Book of Baby and Child Care*), pp. 223–4.
8. Herbert Spencer, *An Autobiography* (London: Williams & Norgate, 1904), vol. 1, pp. 384–5.
9. Herbert Spencer, *First Principles* (London: Watts, 1946; 6th rev. ed.), passim, but see p. 488.
10. Ibid., p. 358.
11. Ibid., app. B, p. 510.
12. Denis C. Phillips, "The Idea of Evolution in Educational Thought," in Edgar L. French, ed., *Melbourne Studies in Education, 1965* (Melbourne: Melbourne University Press, 1966), pp. 93–8.
13. Herbert Spencer, "What Knowledge Is of Most Worth?" in *Essays on Education* (London: Dent, Everyman's Library, 1949), p. 7.
14. Ibid., p. 9.
15. Edward L. Thorndike, *Psychology and the Science of Education* (New York: Teachers College Press, 1962), ed. Geraldine M. Joncich, p. 55.
16. Ibid., p. 60.
17. This movement is discussed in Richard Hofstadter, *Social Darwinism in American Thought* (Boston: Beacon Press, 1955).
18. Wilhelm Rein, *Outlines of Pedagogics* (London: Swan Sonnenschein, 1893), tr. Charles C. and Ida J. van Liew, pp. 97–8.
19. Charles De Garmo, *Herbart and the Herbartians* (London: Heinemann, 1904), p. 109.
20. Ibid., p. 119–20.
21. Cephas Guillet, "Recapitulation and Education," *Pedagogical Seminary* 7 (1900), pp. 422–3.
22. G. Stanley Hall, "Life and Confessions of a Psychologist," selections reprinted in *Health, Growth, and Heredity* (New York: Teachers College Press, 1965), ed. Charles Strickland and Charles Burgess, p. 29.

23. Ibid., p. 32.
24. G. Stanley Hall, "Evolution and Psychology," reprinted in Strickland and Burgess, op. cit., p. 47.
25. G. Stanley Hall, "What We Owe to the Tree-life of Our Ape-like Ancestors," *Pedagogical Seminary* 23 (1916), pp. 94–119.
26. G. Stanley Hall, "The Ideal School as Based on Child Study," reprinted in Strickland and Burgess, op. cit., p. 119.
27. G. Stanley Hall, "The Contents of Children's Minds," reprinted in Wayne Dennis, *Readings in the History of Psychology* (New York: Appleton-Century-Crofts, 1948), p. 275.
28. Ibid., p. 276.
29. Jack London, *The Call of the Wild and Selected Stories* (New York: New American Library, 1960), p. 29. See also pp. 26, 39, 46, 65.
30. G. Stanley Hall, "Childhood and Adolescence," reprinted in Strickland and Burgess, op. cit., p. 103.
31. John Dewey, *The School and Society* (reprinted with *The Child and the Curriculum*; Chicago: University of Chicago Press, Phoenix Books, 1969), p. 48.
32. John Dewey, "Cultural Epoch Theory," in *A Cyclopedia of Education* (New York: Macmillan, 1911), ed. Paul Monroe, vol. 2, p. 241.
33. John Dewey, *Democracy and Education* (New York: Free Press, 1966), p. 72.
34. Ibid., p. 73.
35. Edward L. Thorndike, "Objections to the Theory of Recapitulation," reprinted in Grinder, op. cit., p. 241.
36. Ibid., p. 23.
37. Ibid., p. 244.

5. THE LOSS OF INNOCENCE: THE FREUDIAN CHILD

1. See Bruno Bettelheim, *Freud and Man's Soul* (New York: Knopf, 1983).
2. James Strachey, ed., *The Standard Edition of the Complete Psychological Works of Sigmund Freud*, 23 vols. (London: Hogarth Press, 1966), vol. 16, p. 368.
3. Ibid., vol. 11, p. 38.
4. Jerome Bruner, "Freud and the Image of Man," in F. Cioffi, ed., *Freud* (London: Macmillan, 1973).
5. James A. C. Brown, *Freud and the Post Freudians* (Harmondsworth, Middlesex: Penguin, 1961), p. 18.
6. Strachey, op. cit., vol. 7, p. 233.
7. Ibid., vol. 17, p. 54.
8. Ibid., vol. 20, p. 33.
9. Ibid., p. 217.
10. Ibid., vol. 7, p. 71.
11. Ibid., vol. 15, p. 199.
12. Ibid., vol. 11, p. 46.

13. Ibid., vol. 10, pp. 3–149.
14. Ibid., vol. 13, pp. 130–2.
15. Bruno Bettelheim, op. cit., p. 53.
16. Ibid.
17. Strachey, op. cit., vol. 22, p. 67.
18. Ibid., p. 88.
19. Ibid., p. 156.
20. Ibid., vol. 11, p. 99.
21. Ibid., vol. 7, p. 228.
22. Ibid., vol. 9, p. 237.
23. Ibid., vol. 1, p. 272.
24. Ibid., vol. 7, p. 189.
25. Ibid., vol. 12, p. 254n.
26. Ibid., vol. 9, p. 136.
27. A. S. Neill, *Summerhill* (New York: Hart, 1964), pp. 294–5.
28. Strachey, op. cit., vol. 23, pp. 233–4.
29. Ibid., vol. 19, p. 178.
30. Ibid., vol. 22, p. 129.
31. Ibid., vol. 19, p. 273.
32. Ibid., vol. 10, p. 103.
33. Ibid., vol. 21, pp. 47–8.
34. Ibid., p. 134n.
35. Ibid., vol. 22, p. 151.
36. Ibid., p. 149.
37. Ibid.
38. Ibid.
39. Ibid., vol. 9, p. 36.
40. Ibid.
41. Bettelheim, op. cit., pp. xi, 5.

6. THE AGES OF MAN: FROM GENESIS TO PIAGET

1. William Shakespeare, *As You Like It*, act 2, sc. 7, lines 143–66.
2. A useful survey of these appears in Wayne Dennis, "Historical Beginnings of Child Psychology," *Psychological Bulletin* 46 (1949).
3. Herbert F. Wright, "Observational Child Study," ch. 3, in Paul H. Mussen, ed., *Handbook of Research Methods in Child Development* (New York: John Wiley & Sons, 1960), p. 72.
4. "Tiedemann's Observations on the Development of the Mental Faculties of Children," tr. Carl Murchison and Susanne Langer, *Pedagogical Seminary* 34 (1927), p. 205.
5. John Locke, *An Essay Concerning Human Understanding* (London: Dent, Everyman's Library, 1959), p. 28.
6. Tiedemann, op. cit., p. 206.

7. Ibid., p. 210.
8. Wilhelm Preyer, "Author's Preface to the First Edition," in *The Mind of the Child* (New York: Appleton & Co., 1890), tr. H. W. Brown, p. x.
9. Ibid., p. xiv.
10. Jean Jacques Rousseau, *Emile* (London: Dent, Everyman's Library, 1955), tr. Barbara Foxley, p. 54.
11. Quoted in William Kessen, *The Child* (New York: John Wiley & Sons, 1965), p. 131.
12. For a discussion of Darwin's impact on psychology, see Gardner Murphy, *Psychological Thought from Pythagoras to Freud* (New York: Harcourt, Brace, 1968), ch. 7.
13. Charles Darwin, "A Biographical Sketch of an Infant," *Mind* 2 (1877), p. 19.
14. Kessen, op. cit., p. 118.
15. Rousseau, op. cit., p. 72.
16. Jean Piaget, *Judgment and Reasoning in the Child* (Totowa, N.J.: Littlefield, Adams, 1976), p. 104. (Originally published in English in 1928.)
17. Jean Piaget, *The Construction of Reality in the Child* (New York: Ballantine, 1971), p. 80.
18. Jean Piaget, "Biology and Cognition," in B. Inhelder and H. Chipman, eds., *Piaget and His School* (New York: Springer-Verlag, 1976), p. 45.
19. Jean Piaget, *Psychology of Intelligence* (Totowa, N.J.: Littlefield, Adams, 1969), p. 123.
20. John Flavell, *The Developmental Psychology of Jean Piaget* (New York: Van Nostrand, 1963), p. 24.
21. Erik H. Erikson, *Childhood and Society* (Harmondsworth, Middlesex: Penguin, 1970; reprint), p. 260.
22. For a readable discussion, see Geoffrey Brown and Charles Desforges, *Piaget's Theory: A Psychological Critique* (London: Routledge & Kegan Paul, 1979).
23. See Peter Bryant, *Perception and Understanding in Young Children* (New York: Basic Books, 1974).
24. Karl Popper, *Conjectures and Refutations* (London: Routledge & Kegan Paul, 1965), pp. 33–7.
25. Dylan Thomas, *Quite Early One Morning* (London: Dent, 1957), pp. 83–4.
26. Herbert Ginsburg and Sylvia Opper, *Piaget's Theory of Intellectual Development: An Introduction* (Englewood Cliffs, N.J.: Prentice-Hall, 1969), p. 71.
27. Jerome Kagan, *The Nature of the Child* (New York: Basic Books, 1984), p. 42.
28. Benjamin Spock, *Baby and Child Care* (New York: Pocket Books, 1963; 127th printing of the new ed. of *The Pocket Book of Baby and Child Care*), p. 42.
29. Ibid., p. 260.
30. Ibid., p. 353.
31. Ibid., p. 4.
32. Ibid., p. 1.

33. Ibid., p. 2.
34. Benjamin Spock, *Decent and Indecent* (London: Bodley Head, 1970), p. 12.
35. Spock, *Baby and Child Care*, p. 2.
36. Spock, *Decent and Indecent*, p. 12.
37. Spock, *Baby and Child Care*, p. 353.

7. AN UPBRINGING FIT FOR SOCIETY: MARX AND DEWEY

1. Karl Marx, from *Capital*, excerpted in H. Selsam and H. Martel, eds., *Reader in Marxist Philosophy* (New York: International Publishers, 1963), pp. 98–9.
2. Joel Carmichael, *Karl Marx—The Passionate Logician* (London: Rapp & Whiting, 1965), p. 119.
3. John Dewey, "From Absolutism to Experimentalism," in G. P. Adams and W. P. Montague, eds., *Contemporary American Philosophy* (New York: Macmillan, 1962), vol. 2, p. 21.
4. Georg Wilhelm Friedrich Hegel, from *Philosophy of Right and Law*, excerpted in *The Philosophy of Hegel*, C. Friedrich, ed. (New York: Random House, Modern Library, 1954), p. 269.
5. Carmichael, op. cit., p. 52.
6. Ibid., p. 13.
7. Ibid., p. 226.
8. Ibid., p. 101.
9. Karl Marx, "Marx to Annenkov," in *Marx-Engels Collected Works: Correspondence, 1844–51* (London: Lawrence & Wishart, 1982), vol. 38, p. 96.
10. Friedrich Engels, *The Condition of the Working Class in England*, in *Marx-Engels Collected Works: 1844–45* (1976), vol. 4, p. 439.
11. Ibid., p. 440.
12. Ibid.
13. Carmichael, op. cit., p. 183.
14. *Encyclopedia Britannica*, 15th ed., vol. 11, p. 552.
15. Karl Marx, *Kolnische Zeitung*, in *Collected Works: 1835–43* (1975), vol. 1, p. 193.
16. Ibid.
17. Karl Marx, *Capital: A Critique of Political Economy*, 3 vols. (Chicago: C. H. Kerr, 1915), vol. 1, p. 13.
18. Malcolm I. Thomis, *Responses to Industrialization* (London: David & Charles, 1976), p. 65.
19. Ivy Pinchbeck and Margaret Hewitt, *Children in English Society* (London: Routledge & Kegan Paul, 1973), vol. 2, p. 389.
20. Thomis, op. cit., p. 68.
21. Marx, *Capital*, p. 513.
22. Pinchbeck and Hewitt, op. cit., p. 410.

23. Engels, *Condition of the Working Class*, pp. 468–9.
24. Karl Marx, *Neue Rheinische Zeitung*, No. 269, April 11, 1849, in *Collected Works: 1849* (1978), vol. 9, p. 227.
25. Karl Marx and Friedrich Engels, *Manifesto of the Communist Party*, in *Collected Works: 1845–48* (1976), vol. 6, p. 491.
26. Engels, *Condition of the Working Class*, p. 497.
27. Friedrich Engels, "The Ten Hours Question," in *Collected Works: 1849–51* (1978), vol. 10, p. 274.
28. Pinchbeck and Hewitt, op. cit., p. 403.
29. Engels, *Condition of the Working Class*, p. 450.
30. Karl Marx, "Palmerston—The Psychology of the Ruling Class of Great Britain," in *Collected Works, 1855–56* (1980), vol. 14, p. 370.
31. Ibid.
32. Friedrich Engels, "The English Ten Hours Bill," in *Collected Works: 1849–51*, p. 291.
33. Friedrich Engels, *Condition of the Working Class*, p. 582.
34. Thomis, op. cit., p. 67.
35. Ibid., p. 68.
36. Engels, *Condition of the Working Class*, p. 458.
37. Thomis, op. cit., p. 68.
38. Engels, *Condition of the Working Class*, p. 407.
39. Ibid., p. 409.
40. Ibid.
41. Karl Marx, "The State of British Manufacturers," in *Collected Works: 1858–60* (1980), vol. 16, p. 195.
42. Friedrich Engels, "Speeches in Elberfeld," in *Collected Works: 1844–45*, p. 253.
43. Karl Marx, *Neue Rheinische Zeitung*, No. 201, January 21, 1849, in *Collected Works: 1848–49* (1977), vol. 8, p. 260.
44. Friedrich Engels, "Letters from Wuppertal," *Telegraph für Deutschland*, No. 57, April 1839, in *Collected Works: 1838–42* (1975), vol. 2, p. 19.
45. Karl Marx, "The English Middle Class," in *Collected Works: 1854–55* (1980), vol. 13, pp. 663–4.
46. John Butt, ed., *Robert Owen, Prince of Cotton Spinners* (Newton Abbot: David & Charles, 1971), p. 33.
47. Ibid., p. 71.
48. Ibid., p. 23.
49. Ibid., p. 26.
50. Marx, *Capital*, p. 439.
51. Ibid., p. 529.
52. Ibid., p. 11.
53. Ibid., pp. 529–30.
54. See, for example, Richard Rorty, *Philosophy and the Mirror of Nature* (Princeton, N.J.: Princeton University Press, 1979).
55. John Dewey, *Impressions of Soviet Russia and the Revolutionary World* (New York: New Republic, 1929), p. 10.

56. See Lawrence Cremin, *The Transformation of the School* (New York: Vintage, 1964).
57. John Dewey, *Democracy and Education* (New York: Free Press, 1966), p. iii.
58. John Dewey, *Soviet Russia and the Revolutionary World*, p. 129.
59. John Dewey, "My Pedagogic Creed," reprinted in R. Archambault, ed., *John Dewey on Education* (New York: Modern Library, 1964), pp. 429–30.
60. John Dewey, *Philosophy of Education/Problems of Men* (Paterson, N.J.: Littlefield, Adams, 1964), p. 108.
61. John Dewey, *The School and Society* (reprinted with *The Child and the Curriculum*; Chicago, University of Chicago Press, Phoenix Books, 1969), pp. 10–11.
62. John Dewey, *Soviet Russia and the Revolutionary World*, p. 90.
63. Milford Spiro, *Children of the Kibbutz* (Cambridge, Mass.: Harvard University Press, 1975); and Bruno Bettelheim, *Children of the Dream* (New York: Avon, 1969).
64. John Dewey, *The School and Society*, p. 31.
65. John Dewey, *Democracy and Education*, p. 140.
66. John Dewey, *The School and Society*, p. 35.
67. Ibid., p. 18.
68. Ibid., p. 29.
69. Ibid., p. 14.
70. John Dewey, *Democracy and Education*, p. 320.

8. THE CONDITIONED CHILD

1. Quoted in Robert S. Woodworth, *Contemporary Schools of Psychology*, 8th ed. (London: Methuen, 1952), p. 93.
2. Aldous Huxley, *Brave New World* (Harmondsworth, Middlesex: Penguin, 1958), p. 28.
3. Ibid., p. 29.
4. John B. Watson, *Behaviorism* (Chicago: University of Chicago Press, Phoenix Books, 1966; reprint), pp. 159ff.
5. Huxley, op. cit., p. 12.
6. Watson, op. cit., p. 303.
7. See the papers by Fechner (1860), Wundt (1873), and their students reprinted in Wayne Dennis, ed., *Readings in the History of Psychology* (New York: Appleton-Century-Crofts, 1948).
8. John B. Watson, "Psychology as the Behaviorist Views It" (1913), reprinted in Dennis, op. cit., p. 461.
9. Descartes was a source of this idea in modern thought. See Denis C. Phillips, "James, Dewey, and the Reflex Arc," in *Journal of the History of Ideas* 32 (1971), pp. 555–68, and also the discussion in Chapter 9.
10. Watson, "Psychology as the Behaviorist Views It," p. 457.

11. C. Lloyd Morgan, *An Introduction to Comparative Psychology* (London: W. Scott, 1894), p. 53.
12. Watson, "Psychology as the Behaviorist Views It," pp. 469–70.
13. B. F. Skinner, "How to Teach Animals," reprinted in his *Cumulative Record*, enlarged ed. (New York: Appleton-Century-Crofts, 1961), pp. 412–19. The article originally appeared in *Scientific American* (1951).
14. John B. Watson, *Psychological Care of Infant and Child* (London: Allen & Unwin, 1928), p. 16.
15. William James, *Varieties of Religious Experience* (London: Collins-Fontana, 1960), lectures 7–8.
16. Huxley, op. cit., p. 168.
17. Watson, *Behaviorism*, p. 270.
18. Ibid., p. 104.
19. Watson, *Psychological Care of Infant and Child*, p. 18.
20. Ibid., p. 11.
21. Ibid., p. 13.
22. Ibid., p. 32.
23. Ibid., p. 27.
24. Ibid., p. 28.
25. Ibid., p. 73.
26. Ibid., p. 51.
27. Edward L. Thorndike, "Animal Intelligence" (1898), reprinted in Dennis, op. cit., pp. 377–87.
28. Watson, *Behaviorism*, p. 23.
29. Watson, *Psychological Care of Infant and Child*, pp. 51–3.
30. Ibid., pp. 51–5.
31. Watson, *Behaviorism*, pp. 38–9.
32. B. F. Skinner, "A Case History in Scientific Method," reprinted in his *Cumulative Record*, pp. 79–80.
33. Bertrand Russell, *An Outline of Philosophy* (London: Allen & Unwin, 1948; reprint).
34. B. F. Skinner, "Baby in a Box," reprinted in his *Cumulative Record*, pp. 419–20.
35. Ibid., p. 65.
36. B. F. Skinner, *Science and Human Behavior* (New York: Free Press, 1965), p. 56.
37. Ibid., p. 65.
38. B. F. Skinner, "Reinforcement Today," reprinted in his *Cumulative Record*, p. 132.
39. Skinner, *Science and Human Behavior*, p. 66.
40. B. F. Skinner, *Beyond Freedom and Dignity* (London: Jonathan Cape, 1972), p. 21.
41. Bruno Bettelheim, *Children of the Dream* (New York: Avon, 1969).
42. B. F. Skinner, *Walden Two* (New York: Macmillan, 1962; reprint), p. 256.
43. Ibid., p. 257.

44. Jerome Kagan, *The Nature of the Child* (New York: Basic Books, 1984), p. 279.
45. Carl Rogers, "Toward a Science of the Person," in T. W. Wann, ed., *Behaviorism and Phenomenology* (Chicago: University of Chicago Press, 1964), p. 111.
46. Ibid., p. 119.
47. Ibid., p. 129.
48. Ibid.
49. For a discussion of these three alternatives, and others, see Richard Taylor, *Metaphysics*, 2d ed. (Englewood Cliffs, N.J.: Prentice-Hall, 1974).
50. B. F. Skinner, in the discussion following Rogers's paper, reported in Wann, op. cit., p. 135.
51. Ibid.

9. THE THINKING MACHINE

1. René Descartes, excerpted in Anthony Flew, ed., *Body, Mind, and Death* (New York: Macmillan, 1964), p. 126.
2. Ibid., p. 127.
3. Thomas H. Huxley, excerpted in Flew, op. cit., p. 202.
4. Julian Offray de la Mettrie, *Man a Machine* (La Salle, Ill.: Open Court, n.d.), pp. 143–4.
5. J. David Bolter, *Turing's Man* (Chapel Hill: University of North Carolina Press, 1984), p. 12.
6. Alan M. Turing's "Computing Machinery and Intelligence" is reprinted, with a few other classic papers on the same topic, in Alan Ross Anderson, ed., *Minds and Machines* (Englewood Cliffs, N.J.: Prentice-Hall, 1964), pp. 4–30.
7. Turing, "Computing Machines and Intelligence," p. 14.
8. Ibid., pp. 26–7.
9. Keith Gunderson, "The Imitation Game," in Anderson, op. cit., pp. 60–71.
10. G. Miller, E. Galanter, and K. Pribram, *Plans and the Structure of Behavior* (New York: Holt, 1960).
11. Roy Lachman, Janet Lachman, and Earl Butterfield, *Cognitive Psychology and Information Processing: An Introduction* (Hillsdale, N.J.: Lawrence Erlbaum Associates, 1979), p. 110.
12. Jerry Fodor, *The Language of Thought* (Cambridge, Mass.: Harvard University Press, 1979).
13. Noam Chomsky, *Language and Responsibility* (New York: Pantheon, 1979), p. 98.
14. Herbert Simon, *The Sciences of the Artificial* (Cambridge, Mass.: MIT Press, 1970), pp. 46, 53.

15. Daniel Dennett has some engaging arguments to dispel this fear. See *Brainstorms* (Montgomery, Vt.: Bradford Books, 1978).
16. Robert J. Sternberg, *Intelligence, Information Processing, and Analogical Reasoning* (Hillsdale, N.J.: Lawrence Erlbaum Associates, 1977).
17. Donald Norman, "What Goes on in the Mind of the Learner," in William McKeachie, ed., *Learning, Cognition, and College Teaching* (San Francisco: Jossey-Bass, 1980), pp. 42–3.

10. POSTSCRIPT

1. W. Goldschmidt, "Foreword," in Carlos Castaneda, *The Teachings of Don Juan* (Berkeley: University of California Press, 1972), pp. vii–viii.
2. Karl Popper, *Conjectures and Refutations* (London: Routledge & Kegan Paul, 1965), p. 38.
3. Donald Schon, *Invention and the Evolution of Ideas* (London: Social Science Paperbacks, Tavistock Publications, 1967), p. 192.
4. See Peter Coveney, *The Image of Childhood* (Harmondsworth, Middlesex: Penguin, 1967).
5. For examples, see John F. Cleverley and Denis C. Phillips, *From Locke to Spock* (Melbourne: Melbourne University Press, 1976), pp. 98–108.
6. For an example, see L. Pierce-Clark, *Lincoln: A Psycho-Biography* (New York: Scribners, 1933), pp. 2–8.
7. Jerome Kagan, *The Nature of the Child* (New York: Basic Books, 1984).

INDEX

Abercrombie, M. L. Johnson, 2
Agency, theory of, 130
Air crib, 124–25, 127
American Journal of Psychology, 50
American Psychological Association, 114
Animal psychology, 116–18, 121, 124, 126
Anxiety, 64–65, 70
Aries, Philippe, 145; *Centuries of Childhood*, 6–7
Arnold, Thomas, 31–32, 40, 57, 77
Average child concept, 14–15

Babbage, Charles, 134
Ballantyne, Robert Michael, *The Coral Island*, 28
Beacon Hill school, 41
Bed-wetting, 68
Behaviorism. *See* Conditioning
Bettelheim, Bruno, 64, 78; *Children of the Dream*, 127
Bible, 33, 48, 93
Biogenetic law, 44, 47, 52
Birth, 61–62, 70–71
Bisexuality, 74
Blake, William, 145
Bolter, J. David, *Turing's Man*, 134
Boyd, William, *The History of Western Education*, 9
Breuer, Josef, *Studies on Hysteria* (with Freud), 56
Brueghel the Elder, 3
Bruner, Jerome, 55–56
Burt, Sir Cyril, 14

Cabet, Etienne, 105
Capitalism, 100, 101, 104–5

Castaneda, Carlos, *The Teachings of Don Juan*, 142–43
Castration complex, 58, 73
Child care, 25–27
Child development, 50, 52–53, 80–96; cognitive, 85–89; evaluating studies on, 89–93, 95–96; evolution theory and, 83–85, 90, 94; information processing approach to, 135–40; permissiveness and, 94–95; psychoanalytic theory and, 88–89, 90, 91, 95
Child labor, 101–5; education and, 104–5, 106–7; physical effects of, 102–4
Chomsky, Noam, 137–38
Clark, Edward, 15
Clinical interview, 86
Communism, 99, 103, 105, 107, 108
Compton lectures (Simon), 138
Computers, 131–40; humans mimicked by, 132–40; language of, 132, 135, 136, 137; programs for, 132, 135, 139
Comte, Auguste, 81
Condillac, Etienne Bonnot de, *Treatise on the Sensations*, 18–19
Conditioning, 114–30; animal psychology and, 116–18, 121, 124, 126; classical, 122–23, 124, 125, 126; determinism and, 118–20, 121, 126–30; environment and, 118, 120–21, 124–25, 126–27; of fear, 121, 122; operant, 125–26; opponents of, 114–16, 129–30
Corporal punishment, 31–32, 33–34, 40, 72, 77
Crying, 29, 33, 35–36, 72, 95
Cultural epochs, theory of, 47–52; child growth and, 50, 53; education and, 48–52; history of, 47–48; as school curricula basis, 48–49

Darwin, Charles, 49, 83–85, 89–90, 99, 111, 133; "A Biographical Sketch of an Infant," 84; *The Descent of Man*, 84; *The Expression of the Emotions in Man and Animals*, 84; *On the Origin of Species*, 42, 43, 45, 83–84, 107, 117
Darwin, Erasmus, 36
da Vinci, Leonardo, 63, 66
Day, Thomas, 36, 37
Declaration of Independence, U.S., 119
Defoe, Daniel, *Robinson Crusoe*, 48
Delinquency, 71–72
de Mause, Lloyd, 7–8
Descartes, René, 132–33, 134
Determinism: conditioning and, 118–20, 121, 126–30; free will vs., 127–28, 130; opponents of, 129–30
Dewey, John, 51–52, 97, 98, 107–13, 140, 142; *The Child and the Curriculum*, 108; *Democracy and Education*, 52, 108; *Experience and Nature*, 108; *Interest and Effort in Education*, 108; *The School and Society*, 51–52, 108
Dialectical process, 97, 98, 108
Dickens, Charles, 145
Dream analysis, 59–60, 65
Dualisms, resolution of, 98, 108, 109

Eddington, Sir Arthur Stanley, 91
Edgeworth, Richard, 36–37
Education: for child workers, 104–5, 106–7; cultural-epochs theory and, 48–52; curriculum and, 48–49, 108–9, 111–13, 140; democracy and, 108, 109; of disadvantaged, 13, 14, 26; environmentalist notion of, 20–21, 26–27, 35–36, 38, 41, 86–87, 89, 105–6; as experience, 16–17, 18, 20–21, 26, 35, 144; freedom in, 35–41, 113; hereditarian position on, 26; information processing approach to, 140; naturalism in, 34–41; perfection and, 19–20, 23–24; psychoanalysis and, 74–77; racial recapitulation and, 44–47, 51–53; reform in, 110–13; religious influence on, 28–35, 37, 38, 40–41, 75; restriction and repression in, 28–34, 35, 37, 38, 39–40, 41; sex, 69–71; socialist vs. capitalist, 104–5, 106–7; socially useful, 101, 105–7, 110; training value of, 23–24, 25; utopian, 105–7, 127
Effect, law of, 121, 122
Ego, 63, 64, 65
Ego integrity, 88–89, 90
Einstein, Albert, 91
ELIZA, 132, 135

Embryology, 42–43, 45, 47, 48
Engels, Friedrich, 99–105, 106, 110; *The Condition of the Working Class in England*, 99
Environment, 13–27; conditioning and, 118, 120–21, 124–25, 126–27; education and, 20–21, 26–27, 35–36, 38, 41, 86–87, 89, 105–6; intelligence and, 14–15, 18, 19, 20; parents and, 120–23, 125
Erikson, Erik, 88–90, 91, 146
Evolution, theory of, 42–43, 45–47, 49; child development and, 83–85, 90, 94
Eysenck, Hans J., 14, 16, 19, 25–27; *Race, Intelligence, and Education*, 13

Factory Acts, 102, 103–4, 106
Factory system, 100, 102–4, 106
Family: children and, 6–8, 61–62, 63, 65–68, 94, 111; economics and, 100–103
Family Life, 32, 38
Fast-process research, 139
Feuerbach, Ludwig Andreas von, 99
Firestone, Shulamith, 12
Fodor, Jerry, 137
Fourier, Charles, 105
Freud, Anna, 75
Freud, Sigmund, 5–6, 11–12, 39, 50, 54–79, 91, 95, 129, 130, 132, 137, 142, 145, 146; *Autobiography*, 58; *Dora*, 58–59; *The Ego and the Id*, 63; *Studies on Hysteria* (with Breuer), 56; *Three Essays on the Theory of Sexuality*, 57

Galanter, E., 136
Gall, Franz Joseph, 24
Gladman, F. J., *School Work*, 21
Goethe, Johann Wolfgang von, 66, 71
Golding, William, 38; *Lord of the Flies*, 28
Goldschmidt, Walter, 142–43
Greer, Germaine, 11; *The Female Eunuch*, 12; *Sex and Destiny*, 8
Gregory, Richard L., 2

Haeckel, Ernst, 43–44, 47, 48, 51, 54
Hall, G. Stanley, 49–51, 52, 55; "The Contents of Children's Minds," 50–51; "What We Owe to the Tree-life of Our Ape-like Ancestors," 50
Hamilton, Sir William, 23
Harvard Educational Review, 13
Hazlitt, William, 36
Hegel, Georg Wilhelm Friedrich, 97–98, 99, 107–10, 111
Helmholz, Hermann von, 55, 132

Helvétius, Claude Adrien, 19–20, 26, 99, 146
Herbart, Johann Friedrich, 47, 48, 83
Herbart Club, 48, 51
Heredity, 26–27; intelligence and, 14–15, 16, 17–19
Herschel, Sir John, 3
Homosexuality, 61, 66–67
Hull, Clark L., 121–22
Hume, David, 46, 99
Huxley, Aldous, 116, 128; *Brave New World*, 114–15, 118–19
Huxley, Thomas H., 133

Id, 63, 64
Indeterminism, 129. *See also* Determinism
Individual vs. society, 109–10
Industrial Revolution, 101–2, 104
Infantile sexuality, theory of, 56–58, 69
Instinct, 117, 120
Intelligence, 50; environment and, 14–15, 18, 19, 20; heredity and, 14–15, 16, 17–19; inborn vs. experiential, 16, 38–39; race and, 13, 14, 15
Introspection, 116

James, Henry, 145
James, William, 49, 118
Jensen, Arthur R., 13–15, 16, 18, 19, 25–26, 27; "How Much Can We Boost IQ and Scholastic Achievement?" 13–14
Jesus, 100
Johnson, Lyndon, 13
Journal of Genetic Psychology, 49

Kagan, Jerome, 93, 130, 146; *The Nature of the Child*, 129
Kibbutzim, 110, 127
Kipling, Rudyard, 21
Kissing, 121
Klein, Melanie, 75
Kuhn, Thomas S., 5–6

Laboratory School, 51–52, 107
Ladies Home Journal, 124–25
Lamb, Charles, 36
La Mettrie, Julian Offray De, 133
Lane, Homer, 38
Language: acquisition of, 137–38; computer, 132, 135, 136, 137
Leeds Mercury, 103
Leibniz, Gottfried Wilhelm, 83
Little Commonwealth, The, 38

Little Hans, 71, 75
Locke, John, 15–18, 19, 20–21, 22–23, 25–26, 35, 41, 42, 82, 83, 86, 90, 99, 116, 119, 121, 124, 129, 137, 140, 142, 144; *An Essay Concerning Human Understanding*, 15, 16–17, 21; *Of the Conduct of the Understanding*, 23; *Some Thoughts Concerning Education*, 15–16, 17–18
London, Jack, *The Call of the Wild*, 51
Love, 120

Marcuse, Herbert, 44, 53
Marx, Jenny, 100
Marx, Karl, 91, 97–107, 110, 111, 112, 142; *Capital: A Critique of Political Economy*, 99, 105, 106; *Communist Manifesto*, 106
Masochism, 72
Masturbation, 39, 61, 68–69, 72–73
Mather, Cotton, 30–31, 57
Memory, 136, 138, 140
Miller, G., 136
Mind, 84, 134
Montesquieu, Baron de, 105
Montessori, Maria, 21
"Moral Majority," 32
More, Hannah, 37, 38
Morgan, Lloyd, 117
Muller, Fritz, 43–44

National Society for the Study of Education (N.S.S.E.), 48
Neill, A. S., 4–5, 38–40, 70–71, 72, 75
Neurosthenia, 69
New Lanark, 105, 106
Newman, John Henry Cardinal, 23–24
Norman, Donald, 140, 142

Object lessons, 21–23, 101
Object-permanence notion, 86–87, 93
Observation, 82, 84; of children, 2–3, 4–5, 6–12, knowledge and, 1–3
Obsessional neuroses, 68, 70
Oedipus complex, 56, 57–58, 69, 74; in females, 72–73; guilt and, 58, 63–64, 75
Original sin, 28–35, 37, 38, 75; goodness vs., 34–41, 60–62
Owen, Robert, 99, 105–7

Panoplist, and Missionary Magazine, 34
Paradigms, 5–12, 81, 141–42; evaluation of, 142–44; metaphysical, 143–44; shifts in, 6–7, 11–12; transmission of, 144–46

Parallelism, theory of. *See* Racial recapitulation, theory of
Parents, 66–68; children vs., 6–8, 83, 84, 85–86, 94, 102, 103, 145; disciplinary methods of, 30–32, 33–34, 72; environment provided by, 120–23, 125
Parsimony, law of ("Lloyd Morgan's Canon"), 117
Pavlov, Ivan, 121, 122, 124
Pedagogical Seminary, 49
Perception. *See* Observation
PERDIX, 132, 135, 139
Pestalozzi, Johann Heinrich, 21
Pfister, Oskar, 75
Phrenology, 24–25
Piaget, Jean, 51, 83, 85–90, 91–93, 111, 129, 137, 138, 140, 142, 146
Pitt, William, 101
Plain Truth About Child Rearing, The, 32–33, 38
Plato, *Republic*, 10
Popper, Sir Karl, 88, 90–91, 143–44
Postman, Neil, *The Disappearance of Childhood*, 8
Pragmatism, 107
Preyer, Wilhelm, 82–85, 89–90; *The Mind of the Child*, 82–83
Pribram, K., 136
Progressive movement, 107, 113
Proverbs, 33
Psychoanalysis, 54–56, 61, 64, 68, 78; child development and, 88–89, 90, 91, 95; continuities established by, 56; education and, 74–77
Puberty, 57, 67, 74, 93

Racial recapitulation, theory of, 42–47, 58, 60, 72, 94; education and, 44–47, 51–53. *See also* Cultural epochs, theory of
Reflection, 16–17, 18, 20–21
Reflex actions, 82, 84, 86, 87, 117, 125
Rein, Wilhelm, 47–48, 51
Relativity, theory of, 91
Robespierre, Maximilien de, 40
Robinson, John, 33
Rogers, Carl, 129–30
Romanes, George, 117
Rousseau, Jean Jacques, 11, 39–41, 59, 72, 73, 75, 77, 81, 83, 85, 99, 106, 109, 111, 113, 145; *Emile*, 34–36, 37–38
Russell, Bertrand, 40–41, 123–24, 125; *An Outline of Philosophy*, 124

Sadism, 69, 74
Saint-Simon, Comte de, 105

Schon, Donald, 144
Seduction theory, 56
Selkirk, Alexander, 109
Sensation, 16, 18, 20–21
"Sesame Street," 26
Settlement house movement, 107
Sex education, 69–71
Sexual intercourse, 62, 71
Sexuality, 56–59, 61–64, 68–75, 78; birth and, 61–62, 70–71; crises in, 72–74; delinquency and, 71–72; guilt and, 58, 63–64, 75; of infants, 56–58, 69; innocence and, 60–62
Sexual theorizing, 62–63
Shaftesbury, seventh earl of, 103
Shakers (American), 105
Shakespeare, William, 99; *As You Like It*, 80–81
Shaw, George Bernard, *Pygmalion*, 19
Shelley, Percy Bysshe, 103
Sheppard, Jack, 104
Simon, Herbert, 135–36, 138
Simon and Binet intelligence test, 85–86
Skinner, B. F., 115, 118, 121–22, 123–28, 129, 130, 142, 144–45; *Walden Two*, 127–28
Skinner box, 124
Social Darwinism, 47
Social deprivation hypothesis, 14, 15
Socialism, 99, 104
Society: children and, 6–8, 10, 14, 15, 67–68, 89, 101–5, 109, 120, 127, 146; economics and, 99–100, 101, 104; individual and, 97–98, 101, 105, 109–10; schools and, 110–13; women in, 9–12, 30
Socrates, 10
Sommerville, John, *The Rise and Fall of Childhood*, 8
Spence, Kenneth, 121–22
Spencer, Herbert, 24–25, 44–47, 49, 51, 54; *Essays on Education*, 46, 47; *System of Synthetic Philosophy*, 45; "What Knowledge Is of Most Worth?" 46
Spock, Benjamin, 44, 53; *Baby and Child Care*, 93–96; *Decent and Indecent*, 95
Spurzheim, Johann Kaspar, 24
Stanley, Dean, 31–32, 40
Sternberg, Robert, 139–40
Stimulus substitution, 122–23, 125
Stirling, J. H., *The Secret of Hegel*, 97
Summerhill School, 4, 38, 39, 70–71
Superego, 63–64, 65, 73
Suransky, Dorothy, *The Erosion of Childhood*, 8
Suttie, Ian, 11

Taine, Hippolyte Adolphe, 84
Teaching, 50, 106, 111; of object lessons, 21–22; from particular to general, 47
Testing: of intelligence, 85–86, 92; prediction and, 90–92; of theories, 90–93
Textbooks, 22, 106
Theoretical models, 3–5, 64, 81. *See also* Paradigms
Thomas, Dylan, "Return Journey", 92
Thorndike, E. L., 46–47, 52–53, 121–23, 124, 125
Thumb sucking, 32–33
Thurber, James, 1
Tiedemann, Dietrich, 81–83, 84–85, 89–90, 118
Time sampling, 82
Toilet training, 68, 95
Tom Brown's Schooldays, 40
Totalitarianism, 115
Turing, Alan M., 133–36, 140; "Computing Machinery and Intelligence," 134–35; "On Computable Numbers,"

Turing, Alan M. *continued* 133–34
Turing machine, 133–34, 136
Turpin, Dick, 104
Twain, Mark, 145

Ure, Andrew, 103

Voltaire, 37, 99
von Baer, Karl Ernst, 42, 43, 45, 47

"War on Poverty," 105
Watson, John B., 114–24, 126, 128; *Behaviorism*, 114, 119
Weizenbaum, Joseph, 132
Wesley, John, 28–30, 33, 37, 38, 57, 73, 111
Wesley, Susanna, 28–29, 33–34, 38, 57
Wollstonecraft, Mary, 36
Wordsworth, William, 145
Wundt, Wilhelm, 49

Ziller, Tuiskon, 47, 48, 51

ABOUT THE AUTHORS

JOHN CLEVERLEY taught in elementary schools in Australia before receiving his Ph.D. from the University of Sydney in the history of nineteenth-century education. His earliest writing focused upon the rearing of children in the newly founded Australian colonies. He developed an interest in comparative education, and has traveled widely in the Soviet Union, China, and Thailand, and he has been an advisor to the government of Papua New Guinea. He has edited a number of books on the history of Australian education; his other volumes include *The First Generation* (1971) and *The Schooling of China* (1985). He was coauthor, with D. C. Phillips, of *From Locke to Spock* (1976). Professor Cleverley has taught in universities in the United States and Australia, and currently is head of the Department of Social and Policy Studies in Education at the University of Sydney.

D. C. PHILLIPS taught in high schools and universities in Australia before moving to the United States in 1974. Currently he is Professor of Education and Philosophy at Stanford University. His main interests are in philosophy of social science, educational and psychological research methodology, and history of nineteenth- and twentieth-century thought. He has published in a variety of journals including *Psychological Review, Educational Psychologist, Journal of the History of Ideas*, and *Harvard Educational Review*. Professor Phillips was coauthor, with Lee J. Cronbach and others, of *Toward Reform of Program Evaluation* (1980); his other books include *Holistic Thought in Social Science* (1976) and *Perspectives on Learning* (1985; with Jonas Soltis).